THE
WOLCOTT
CIRCUS

THE
WOLCOTT
CIRCUS

MICHAEL SNARR

gatekeeper press™
Columbus, Ohio

The Wolcott Circus

Published by Gatekeeper Press
2167 Stringtown Rd, Suite 109
Columbus, OH 43123-2989
www.GatekeeperPress.com

This publication is designed to provide accurate and authoritative information in regard to the subject matter covered. It is sold with the understanding that the publisher is not engaged in rendering legal or accounting services. If legal advice or other expert assistance is required, the services of a competent professional person should be sought.

Library of Congress Control Number: 2020951424

ISBN (hardcover): 9781662907708

ISBN (paperback): 9781662907715

eISBN: 9781662907722

Printed in the United States of America

Dedication

To all the men
of Pi Kappa Alpha
who lived through the Sixties with me
and made my life so much the better for it.
Phi-Phi-K-A

Contents

Contents

Author's Note

IN 1960, THE USA heard Julie Andrews sing "the hills are alive with the sound of music" more than any other lyric, and *The Sound of Music* was the number one album of the year. In 1968, the number one most listened-to album in the country was *Are You Experienced?* by Jimi Hendrix. "Manic Depression" was one of the hits from that album.

In less than a decade a lot changed. And not just our taste in music . . .

(I listened to Jimi a lot more than Julie, in case you were wondering.)

Introduction

L ET ME TELL you about the amazing world I grew up in. It was innocent, idyllic and hopeful, and at the same time eye-opening, foreboding and perhaps even a little frightening.

The world was full of experiences that transformed my life and changed me forever. And not just me. The Sixties and early Seventies had a far-reaching effect on those of us who lived in that world during our teens and twenties.

In grade school, we played in the streets until very, very late at night without our mothers worrying. We walked or rode bicycles everywhere. I remember hearing about the first murder in my town, sometime in the late '50s or early '60s, which seemed almost impossible to imagine. We soon forgot about it.

In high school, we often "dragged State Street" looking for girls. Or, we wore football helmets and had food fights using odiferous produce. We plucked the discarded food from the back of grocery store dumpsters and loaded it into a couple of pickup trucks, subsequently squaring off in school parking lots, playgrounds or golf courses late at night. We took on neighboring schools or upper classmen at our own high school. We threw eggs and tomatoes and crushed cantaloupes over the football helmets of our rivals. And vice-versa. The police almost always came, brandishing flashlights and threatening to shoot if we didn't stop in our tracks but never drawing their weapons, and who behaved more like an updated version of the Keystone Cops from the silent movies of the Twenties. I once watched a fellow classmate whose father would someday become the governor of Utah, captured and tossed into the back of a police car. With some ingenuity, he slid across the seat of the car, its blinding red and blue lights flashing on top, then stepped out the other side, and tried to disappear into the night next to me. Before it was over, both of us better understood the definition of the word "adrenaline." As I cut through someone's yard and hurdled over their backyard fence, I heard a policeman say, "Stop or I'll shoot!" But he didn't.

We were a nuisance, not a threat. We were there to have fun. I halfway think the police were there for the same reason. Something to do.

We had foot races in Dave Boyce's neighborhood; not against each other, but against Dave's father's Ford Comet, one of the first of the new "gas saving" vehicles that were becoming popular at the time. The Edsel and other gas behemoths were vanishing, and these new "compacts" were slow afoot. Especially Dave's Comet. So, four or five of us would line up on an imaginary starting line as Dave revved up the Comet in the middle of the street. When one of our arms signaled it, the race began. The goal was to beat the Comet for about 50 yards or so down Berkeley Avenue. We often did, to Dave's dismay. I still can't understand how Ford had the audacity to name their economy car a "Comet."

Or, we might play "Over the Line" baseball at a playground, or even in the streets. Sometimes we used tennis balls and played "Home Run Derby." A homerun was a ball that sailed over the neighbor's house. A ball that failed to clear the house often spelled the end of the game, especially if it hit the house in a vulnerable spot, like a window.

We also played tennis and golf in the heat of the summer, snuck into church gyms to play basketball, snuggled with young fresh-faced girls in their front yards, or the back seats of someone's car, or in the darkened basements of unsuspecting parents where we spun Johnny Mathis LPs. We packed the bleachers at high school football games, ate hamburgers, fries and shakes at local hamburger drive-ins (complete with car hop service), and worried about the emergence of the teenage curse called "zits" in prominent places on our faces, usually arriving just before the Prom or a first date.

Life was good.

So was school. Not the homework part, and not always the classroom; but I loved my classmates. Everyone seemed to get along. There was little jostling for territory. We were a pretty tight group. Richard "Bird" Morgan made high school life even better. He rode his Vespa motor scooter down the hallways, and even down the stairs near the foyer. He drove his refurbished car (complete with a chair from one of our classrooms) backwards to school because it only worked in reverse. He opened the door of my English class one day and rolled a shotput across the floor. I was seated on the front row, and I watched it slow to a halt just to the right of the teacher's desk. All eyes were on the shotput, including Mr. Nance's, our now befuddled instructor. We were supposed to be quietly studying at the time, so he calmly picked it up and placed it on his desk. About 20 minutes later, one of the school's office support staff, a student, entered the room and presented a "pink slip" to the teacher. It simply said "shotput," with a box checked that read "report to the office." The teacher, still calm and collected, simply shook his head no.

Short and just a touch stocky, "Bird" was the unofficial school mascot. He was a hit. With everyone. You might see him at a football game wearing a gas mask, or tossing his drink and bag of popcorn on a movie audience, or playing dead on the side of the road. It was rumored that he occasionally appeared naked after flagging down a tennis ball in a neighbor's bushes during an over-the-line game. He epitomized what it was like to live high school life in the '60s. Then there was Kent Murdock, future president of a Fortune 500 company, along with Rex Johnson stealing a sculpture of Dr. Arbogast, the school's first principal, right out of the foyer in plain daylight. They paid penance by cleaning the school parking lot after classes. The principal didn't seem to notice or care that these two criminals tidied things up wearing only their skivvies. Rex said they got the idea to borrow Arbogast's bust from watching *Topkapi*, a daring heist movie that was popular that year, except those protagonists stole a priceless dagger at night with their pants on.

Anything seemed possible when I attended Highland High School in a Salt Lake City suburb during 1965. To say it was a very good year was probably an understatement.

ONE

Things Change

On May 23, 1974, the Pi Kappa Alpha fraternity house at 51 North Wolcott burned down. It had been my house for the previous six years (I was a slow learner) while I attended the University of Utah trying to get a degree. I shared it with my fraternity brothers between the ages of 19 and 25, or thereabouts, all of us coming and going while we attended college. The house had room for about twenty live-ins, based on seniority, and during my last two years in school, I enjoyed residing there so much that I really didn't want to get a degree. Fortunately, I did graduate, just barely, and was working downtown when I heard the news. Seems the room wallpapered with Coors six-pack cartons caught fire somehow, and those beer cartons almost exploded, sending flames all through the 7,000 square foot home. Luckily, everyone got out alive, even from "Outer Siberia," a makeshift add-on room that appealed to less claustrophobic frat brothers and was probably the location of the fire's genesis. The demise of our beloved edifice gave the perturbed neighbors the opportunity to petition to rezone the neighborhood, thus excluding the chance of rebuilding it as a fraternity house.

The house was originally purchased in 1939, which put it on the first cusp of the golden era of frat life at the University of Utah. Until then, I'm not sure the Pi Kapps had a regular place to meet. That transaction solidified the fraternity as a legitimate entry into Greek life on campus. And it's when the fraternity really started to grow. And grow. And grow. All the way to 1965, when it was widely considered to be among the top fraternities on campus.

What had been my home away from home was architecturally inviting, nestled on a quiet street in an exclusive upscale neighborhood surrounded by other large, beautiful and timeless houses. Large trees and meticulous landscaping made it one of the most inviting and prestigious residential areas in the city. It was an eclectic masterpiece, almost as if Frank Lloyd Wright had orchestrated some of its look and feel.

I never thought of our house as massive even though so many of us lived there. Today, there are two homes where there used to be one. Positioned on a large, round corner linking two other streets, we had plenty of space for an east-facing front entrance and a large, covered patio on the north end. The large living room, where we held meetings for close to 75 men, spilled out onto the patio. A game room, a poker room, a large kitchen and a telephone booth just off the expansive lobby and staircase finished off the main floor. Somehow the builders had managed to sandwich in at least ten bedrooms upstairs along with one or maybe two bathrooms. The yard virtually surrounded the house. Interestingly, there were no locks on any of the doors, including the front door, at any time in our history. We would probably have welcomed most intruders. And who wanted to bother a bunch of fraternity bums in the middle of the night, anyway?

That day, as I walked through the main floor, which had buckled and now looked like a still life painting of broken wooden waves in a shoreline surf, I didn't think about this being the demarcation of my life on campus, or a symbol of how the world would be different going forward, having just passed through one of the most tumultuous periods in US history. Looking back, though, it was both.

That same year, President Nixon was impeached for lying about the Watergate break-in. In its wake was the Vietnam War, AIDS—the most frightening disease since the plague—the Kent State shootings of innocent students by our own military, the explosion of rock and roll music, an increased use of drugs like LSD, the military draft, flag burnings, the rise of the Black Panthers and the Hell's Angels, Woodstock, a societal shift away from coats and ties to bell bottoms, a sexual revolution, an explosion of new music, and a propensity by some to just "drop out" of life, gravitating to places like Height-Ashbury in San Francisco to "make love not war." If that wasn't enough, we even had a flu pandemic that took the lives of about 100,000 Americans. The world had changed dramatically since I pledged to live a frat boy's life back in 1965. None of us could have guessed. Not even Richard M. Nixon.

TWO

Two Lessons

IN 1965, I was a typical high school kid, fighting acne (which had no known cure at the time) with sunlamps and talcum powder, lifting weights in a feeble attempt to bulk up, and eating as many burgers, shakes and fries as I could, which didn't make a dent in my skinny torso. Even regular Friday night dinners at the local pizzeria were inconsequential.

Looking back, I realize these were among the very best times, especially the summers between 8th and 12th grade, even though our parents made us find summer jobs. Sort of. I spent one summer painting fire hydrants (yes, that's the truth) for the SLC Water Department. I was also a lookout on a mountain top, trying to spot fires that might roar through a nearby canyon. My favorite job, though, was cutting the greens at a local golf course. We also raked sand traps, watered fairways and trimmed around trees and bushes, from six in the morning until three in the afternoon, seven days a week. Sometimes we swam in the water hazards, looking for golf balls when our bosses weren't watching. Mostly we worked pretty hard under the beating, bleaching sun, and proudly took our deep, deep suntans to school in the fall, hoping they would endear us to the girls in our classes. This was at least a decade before someone tried to memorialize us in the movie *Caddyshack*.

Best of all, the summer nights were ours. And we made the most of them, walking for hours under trees that spread their limbs across streets and languished over dimmed, ornamental streetlamps. It was almost like walking in a large cavern, with only glowing clouds and moonlight periodically visible between the branches and green leaves, amplified by the distant sound of crickets or a breeze filtering through the trees. It was euphoric, punctuated by a hint of testosterone as we combed the neighborhoods for a certain girl we might hope to see or luckily end up walking with. Who knows, we might even hold hands or hug in the moonlight. We called kisses "wraps" for some reason, and the evening usually ended with this brief query from those who didn't get to peel off from the huddle: "Well, did you get your wraps?"

During the last really blissful summer, between 11th and 12th grade, we were all driving cars, thus creating a new life-altering dynamic. Now we could actually pick up girls, or race Tom Woolf's Volkswagen along one of the thoroughfares on the east side of town. (Utah freeways were mostly still just blueprints at this point.) Once—and this is petrifying to think of now—Tom reached over 75 mph along a two-lane city street, as the rest of us literally gasped for air and prayed that little bug of a car would stay upright or not slam into a tree. Tom was the leader of our quirky little foursome clique which included Rex Johnson (who would someday gain fame as "U-Haul" Johnson), Erv Terry (who I would later compare to Indiana Jones), and me, all of 5 foot 7 and pushing 125 pounds. But of course, I had the sun-bleached hair to hang out of the car. Life was moving fast in more ways than one.

Two defining moments for me, in retrospect, occurred during my tour of duty in high school. I was very happy to walk away in one piece from both of them. Especially the first. It was sort of a "live to tell about it" moment that happened sometime during my junior year, when some classmates and I decided to ride inner tubes down the usually calm stream running through Sugarhouse Park one especially wet spring. It looked easy at first, but soon the stream turned into a gushing torrent that slapped the bank and pushed us along through whitecaps that kept growing. I remember holding onto a tree limb after jettisoning my tube just before an eight-foot drop-off above protruding rocks. I held on literally for dear life, submerged in what might be the first "waterboarding" experiment, as my feet dangled over the jagged rocks below. At that moment, I realized how dear life really is, and how much I wanted to play the rest of it out the best I could. With every bit of strength I had, I managed to pull myself to safety and crawl onto the soggy bank. Gazing over the precipice at the foamy conclusion below, I knew I was a very lucky young man.

The second one happened right after graduating from Highland High School in 1965, when my three compatriots and I decided to take a trip to Laguna Beach, California. Even though I had just had my first knee surgery (after tearing cartilage as I slid into home plate in a softball gym class), we made the trek in Tom's VW, the four of us packed in there along with a couple of swimming suits, t- shirts and cut-off shorts to last each of us a week. It was a trip you could never take today. It's not that we did anything illegal (except con our way past the guards at the Tijuana border at just eighteen years old); it's just that we live in a different world now, and lurking behind playful mischief is trouble. And, a bunch of laws written to protect us. What was once mischief can be called criminal now. In the summer of 1965, though, we slept on the front lawn of the Flamingo Hotel in Las Vegas until Erv and Rex were chased from the hotel swimming pool after hours, looked for the Beach Boys at Laguna Beach, played hoops with local beachcombers, ate a lot of pizza, drank Mexican Cokes at a bar in Tijuana with topless waitresses, and walked back across the border without incident. It was maybe the first rite of passage for me, but I never thought much about what could have easily happened to us until recently.

On Graduation night, I stayed out all night with Barbara Coulam, a cute and vivacious young woman. My good fortune. We celebrated the night with a horde of other graduating seniors. Many had charted out their lives after high school, but I hadn't. It was the first time I actually thought, *what am I going to do now?*

We were exuberant about finishing high school that warm summer night, but the next day was different. It was a day I didn't have to go to school, get a job, or get a life. Of course, I also knew that wasn't the right thing to do. And admittedly, the choices were narrow: find work right away; join the military and probably get shipped to Vietnam; or go to college, get some kind of an education, and meet smart, pretty girls who were going there too. Some of my friends would soon choose to serve our church as missionaries for two years. But that meant getting up every day at 6:00 am, studying scriptures for a couple of hours, knocking on doors all day, and not kissing any girls for two years. I wasn't big on sacrifice. I was big on fun. Easy decision.

A few months later I entered college, and thus began the slow turn from plebian innocence to the gamely pursuit of life. But I'll never forget how much fun we had in high school. Our parents, part of the "Greatest Generation," made sacrifices that guaranteed our freedom, and they probably shook their heads in disbelief at times as they watched us make the most of it.

THREE

Frat Life

ONE OF THE first things I discovered when I enrolled in college was that there was an alternate universe there, where guys (and girls) could get an education (albeit not always in the classroom), make lots of friends, and have lots of fun going to parties, playing sports, and generally hanging around a big house with lots of others while trying to figure out what to do next. In my case, that took almost six years. They called it fraternity and sorority life, and it spoke to me, you might say.

Three of my best friends decided it would be cool to join the Special Forces and jump out of planes for the next six months. So I said goodbye to them, warning them that they might never come back alive. And I joined a fraternity that fall, just as school started to come into view.

I spent the summer getting a suntan at the golf course, eating the famous "Pigs Dinner" at the local ice cream parlor, and dating wonderful girls who, like me, were about to embark on college life. I also attended frat parties and met seasoned college students who raved about their various house cultures.

It didn't take me long to decide I wanted to be one of them.

I also discovered that frat houses weren't just party hangouts for drinkers but also generated jocks and brains, and were mostly filled with ambitious students who wanted to make a mark when they (eventually) left college. Frat houses often led the university in GPA and athletic success via intramurals. Members had pretty girlfriends and seemed like honorable men. I confirmed this as I looked into several houses that summer: not just Pi Kappa Alpha but Sigma Chi, Beta Theta Pi, Kappa Sigma, Sigma Nu and a couple of others. Frat life was for me. I knew that in an instant.

Although the Beatles were the musical sensation of the world, America's Beach Boys modeled the kind of life I wanted to embrace: a carefree, relaxed, laying on the beach kind of life. You could hear their music wafting out of the upstairs windows of fraternity and sorority houses. That was how it felt the fall of 1965. Argyle sweaters were big. Belted corduroy pants were stylish. Short haircuts dotted the campus. Women curled their long hair and wore bangs. And conservative dresses, or maybe even jeans. Men opened doors for their dates, who often sat close to their escort while riding in a parent's car, sliding across the bench seat to snuggle up to the driver. That's how you knew if your date liked you, at least to some degree. You learned to drive with one arm around the girl next to you. Seatbelts were an afterthought, at best.

But the world was tumbling towards a new existence. Music, politics, business and life would soon be changing. The Beach Boys would give way to the Rolling Stones, and things would never be the same. The Beach Boys sang about girls, surfing, living the good life with their parents, and having good vibrations. The Stones and The Doors, on the other hand, sang irreverently about politics, sex, drugs and a life that was filled with danger, fighting in the streets, or knowing that war was "just a shot away." Soon cars would have bucket seats, which led to more socializing in the back seats. The fashion world seemed to turn upside down and inside out at the same time. All kinds of floral shirts became popular for men. Button-down collars and ties almost disappeared. Men's pants seemed to be made with about twice as much fabric. They were called bell bottoms for an obvious reason. Hairstyles changed, too. Short haircuts disappeared. Guys started wearing their hair longer, like girls used to (but without the curlers). Girls started cutting their hair, and new attitudes began emerging about a lot of other things besides fashion. Rules and etiquette seemed to be shifting. But frat boys adjusted. There was opportunity to be had, even if it was coupled with a little uncertainty.

FOUR

College Life

NOTHING COMPARES TO life in college because you're mostly on your own. You can be a straight A student if you work hard enough. You can find and date the one you will marry. You can prepare for life after college. Or, you can do what I did. You can join a fraternity and stretch college out a few more years. You can sleep in, take mostly mid-day or afternoon classes, eat greasy hamburgers at Snappy's, a famous local diner, and visit with frat brothers until 2 a.m. on the front porch or in the front room of the Pi Kappa Alpha house. You can become a gym rat, playing hoops on the open courts at the campus recreation center, fitting in a little studying and time with girls along the way.

I didn't start out that way. No. Certainly not. I had big plans. I was going to do all of the above AND get straight As. Meet the girl I would marry, and launch my career. Maybe run for President. But that all changed when I took my first class, US History 101. It was held at 7:45 a.m. three days a week. At the time, I lived about twenty minutes from campus, plus the time it took to find a parking spot. I'm guessing there were maybe

15,000 of us at the University of Utah that year, and I swear half the student body signed up for that class.

To make matters worse, the class was taught on closed circuit TV. I never met the professor in person, although he had written some book on history and looked very distinguished, standing behind a podium and lecturing us intently via black and white TV monitors. I heard there were about three rooms full of students with televisions positioned strategically throughout. You would think that would be a good thing, and it was in some ways. It didn't really matter what time you showed up. Or even if you showed up at all. That could be a bad thing when it came time to hand out grades. But I promise you, I did my part. I made it to class. I took notes. I read the book. I studied pretty hard. For at least the first half of the semester.

Then it started to snow. Since it was mostly a "commuter campus," people left even earlier for class. Parking spots were harder to come by. Parking tickets not so much. I started attending class without taking a shower, which made it hard to talk to girls and find the one I was going to marry. On really snowy days . . . well, you can guess what happened.

The rest is history. I earned a C+. Further, I can't remember one thing the professor said. Not to this day.

Afternoon classes presented a different problem, especially in the spring and fall, when the weather was simply wonderful. I had to sit through plenty of classes in high school with the windows open and lots of girls running around outside, while I sweltered away in some physics class I had to have to graduate. Why should I do that again? College was ELECTIVE. Using some logic I'd picked up as a freshman in a philosophy class from a white-haired, slightly scruffy professor who didn't seem to have a care in the world, I deduced that the best thing to do, indeed, was to extend my college career a little and take fewer classes each semester, which would give me time to ponder my career and find my true love. I never found a way to thank my brilliant Philosophy professor, but I'm not sure he would have given me better than a C+ grade.

I gave this theory the litmus test one spring when the only time I could schedule a remedial Algebra class I needed in order to graduate was at 3:20 pm on Monday, Wednesday and FRIDAY! The class was held in the Chemistry building for some reason, with no AC, but lots of open windows with the sound of girls laughing and running around in the distance. One day towards the end of the semester, my math teacher, peering over my fellow students in front of me all the way to the back row, asked me my name. All sorts of alarms went off in my head. I'd been there to take the tests but had missed virtually every lecture she'd given. Professors don't take kindly to that, even if you pass all the tests. I couldn't blame her. When I told her who I was, she replied, "I've never seen you before. Your name is here on the roll, and you've taken the tests, but you've never attended my class." I made a feeble attempt to convince her I had been there but recently got a haircut and a shave.

I met with her after class. And I attended the rest of the course, even as the number of girls running around just outside my window near the back door seemed to multiply (simple math) geometrically. Luckily, she took mercy on me, probably because she had been a student once, too . . . only most likely one of those straight-A kind of students you read about. I collected another C+.

Campus life was inviting, especially if it didn't involve attending classes. Or walking to class during rain, hail or snow. Spring and fall were particularly beautiful, and not just due to all the girls walking around. The trees seemed majestic. So did the buildings. The library was always buzzing with a low hum of muffled voices, and people hopping between study cubicles to visit or compare notes. Ear buds hadn't yet been invented, so it was easy to interrupt someone in order to mingle with them. Another great thing was that backpacks weren't stylish yet and briefcases were used only by professors and nerds, so it was key to carry as few books as possible. Between classes you could hang out at the student cafeteria and visit even more. Visiting was encouraged, in fact.

The other option was the fraternity house. When I lived there, I often studied in my room on the second floor overlooking the backyard's grassy lawn and eight-foot basketball hoop, where we dunked not only basketballs but all kinds of other objects. I sometimes shared the room with another brother. It wouldn't take long for a half-dozen of us to begin accumulating in one of the rooms to watch television or make plans for a burger run that night. One evening, in the dead of winter, as I studied some kind of book on anthropology or maybe geometry, Jon "The Heat" Lervig threw three snowballs, lickety-split, into the two-inch gap of my second story bedroom window from about twenty feet away. *Pop. Pop. Pop.* Just like that. We called him "The Heat" because he had reportedly been clocked at 95 mph on a dirt mound, throwing pitches for an AAA baseball team in California. As I peered cautiously out the window, Lervig's ear-to-ear grin lit up the night. It was in this environment that I developed Attention Deficit Disorder.

ADD wasn't my only problem. Some of my classes just didn't make sense. Here's what I mean. I took a Chinese history class taught by a German professor of all people. His name was Helmut something. He spoke with a thick, almost indistinguishable accent and he gave us "fill in the blank" tests which were virtually impossible to decipher. Half the time I couldn't understand what he was saying, and half the time I couldn't follow his sentence structure on his tests. C+.

On the other hand, my photography class was taught by a very communicative professor. The problem here was that it was a night class. My good friend and frat brother U-Haul Johnson took it with me, but missed a lot of the classes and assignments because he was working. So, I took photographs for both of us (yes, that's cheating), and he turned some of my photos in as his. Maybe I should have been more discriminate because those borrowed photos earned him a B in the class. My photos got . . . that's right, a C+.

I took a mythology class with a girl I was quite passionate about at the time. It wasn't just about Zeus and Thor and Ulysses and Neptune and all those other superheroes. It was about Pelias and Theseus, Meleager, Nestor, Cresphontes and Merope and the Heraclid. Daedalus and Icarus showed up, too. Over 400 pages of these guys were crammed into a small black book with exceptionally tiny print and a few drawings of Greek gods doing all kinds of amazing things. I took the class only because my girlfriend was interested in it. We even stayed up all night to study for one of the tests. I liked the idea of an all-nighter but my thinking was only to study some of the time. She was a better student than me. I still have the book, and it looks pretty good and intellectual sitting on one of our bookshelves, but it was a really tough class. Plus, the teacher chewed out my girlfriend and me one day after class for sitting in the back and giggling too much. C+.

I think the real problem with school came down to my brain. I don't think I was wired for getting good grades. My sister was. She would have aced German History and Mythology for sure, and figured out a way to get an A in Photography, too. She could read something once and absorb it, remember it and regurgitate it at a moment's notice. She ended up graduating with honors and got a couple of Master and PHD-type postgraduate degrees after that. I'm not jealous, but it sure would have been handy if I could have just used her brain for studying and taking tests.

I also had frat brothers with brains like hers. Craig Boorman, for instance, could literally sleepwalk through classes and get straight As. He went to law school and sat on the front porch of the frat house almost every day. We were pumping all kinds of geniuses out of the Pi Kapp House while I was there. We even "adopted" a brilliant student who lived close to 51 North Wolcott and often rode his bike along our street. Some of our geniuses took him under their wings and befriended him. He wasn't socially gifted, but his brain worked like no one else's. He actually got so excited while taking final exams that he couldn't contain himself from laughing as he read the test questions.

Some frat houses had a file cabinet full of old tests that anyone could use. I don't think we even bothered with that, and I'm not sure it would have benefited me anyway, because it would just mean I would have to spend more time studying. I yearned for the times Lervig would throw snowballs at my window, interrupting me and giving me an excuse to shelve my Anthropology book for a while. The good thing about school for me was that I figured out how to get a C+ in just about any class. Luckily, the "scholarly" men in my fraternity would help fill in the gaps in my education over the next several years, and leave me with a broader perspective that has helped me throughout my life. I might have been a C+ college student but I think my fraternity brothers would have given me a much better grade in Pi Kappa Alpha.

FIVE

A Most Unusual Cast of Characters

THE FRATERNITY I would join as a freshman plebe had a history of attracting a most unusual cast of characters with diverse backgrounds, beliefs and motivations. Then four to five years later it spat them back out. They landed in a world that really needed them, despite what could have been a somewhat intoxicating fraternity life. Most found themselves entering society in time to meet it head-on. University presidents, corporate presidents, bank presidents, entrepreneurs, ecclesiastical stalwarts, politicians who went all the way to the White House, attorneys, doctors, real estate developers, journalists, military leaders, teachers, laborers, bus drivers and more. Here's a small fragment, an incomplete list, of Pi Kapp brothers I had the good fortune to associate with from my era alone.

Gordy Gee became President of Ohio State University and then West Virginia University. Karl Rove ran the Republican Party during the George W. Bush administration and became his top advisor, too. Nick Rose ran Mountain Fuel, a local public utility. Brian Swinton, who mentored me as a young "PIKE", ran a successful real estate time share development company before settling in with the Marriott Corporation. His younger brother, Jeff, a pledge brother of mine, became a very successful attorney. Don Pugh ran Cummins Diesel. Steve Harmsen, my big brother in the fraternity, has operated a successful family business for 30 years and been active in politics. Craig Zwick and Whit Clayton became full time leaders in the Church of Jesus Christ of Latter-day Saints. Steve Anderson, Erv Terry and Walt Hanni became real estate developers in Alaska.

Lew Bautista started a chain of successful restaurants in Minnesota. Steve Bushnell made millions selling swimming pool covers to William Shatner and other stars in California. John Nordquist, who threw baseballs for the university, became an educator in South Korea and sidelined in some kind of secret work for the government he never talked about (the CIA, I'm guessing). Rod Shelton started a highly successful industrial supply company. Gary Sandberg owned and managed a family mill that did fabulous woodwork for all kinds of businesses and churches. Pat Roylance ran PR for a congressman in Washington. JR Knight started his own financial planning company. Rod Decker, Bob Bernick and Charlie "Bus" Seldin became accomplished writers, journalists and broadcasters. Ray McEvilly served the country as an Air Force intelligence officer. Steve Purhonen became an officer in the Army. Bill Souvall owned a construction firm. Wally Reichert became a brain surgeon. Rich Irion became a successful gynecologist. Brent Gold and Scott Welling became successful attorneys in Park City, a ski resort town about thirty minutes from 51 North Wolcott. Glen Holley, my little brother in the fraternity, went there to build houses. Scott Anderson has been the president of a large regional bank for a number of years. Doug Black was president of another bank in the city. Bob Woolf became a successful orthodontist. Bob Clark, a football star at the university, went into real estate. So did Paul Markosian. Don Brady became a renowned interior designer in Park City. Brent Eldredge owns a high-end retail store called Eldredge Furniture. Ed Muir became a highly regarded history professor at Northwestern University. Ross Anderson was our chapter advisor and ran his own engineering firm. Dan Paxton worked for Pepsico as a senior vice president before starting his own leadership consulting business. Kent Norton became an attorney and then a successful television meteorologist. Wally Boyack worked as an attorney for the Securities and Exchange Commission. Tom Buxton started a cutting-edge gym and workout center. And Nolan Bushnell founded the breakthrough video game company Atari, and then Chuck E. Cheese.

Nolan's story is especially interesting. I've heard he figured out how to invent video games as a part-time employee for a local amusement park. He was in charge of the pinball machine pavilion, and when the machines broke-down he had to fix them. While he attended the university and played cards most nights at the frat house, he found time to build one of the first ever video games. He called it "Pong." Weighing a ton in the large box that housed it, Nolan hoisted it into a truck and talked a local bar into trying it out. A few weeks later, the bar owner told him to get rid of it because it was broken. He was right, it was broken. Jammed full of quarters broken. Pong morphed into the highly successful company Atari. Nolan now lives in Northern California and does pretty much whatever he wants.

One frat brother, who enjoyed a prosperous career, retired and became a bus driver, something he always wanted to do. I saw him one day as I boarded a bus he was driving near the university. He was beaming. It was clear to me he loved his job, probably as much as anyone.

During my college career I bet I've met over 500 Pi Kapps who became highly successful members of society. I know I've overlooked or forgotten many, many game changers from Alpha Tau, local chapter of Pi Kappa Alpha. Stephen Covey, entrepreneur and author of *The 7 Habits of Highly Effective People*, and a Pi Kapp at the University of Utah in the '50s, said it best: "To have the best future, create it."

SIX

The Wanderer

I MET ERV TERRY in fifth grade. I overheard a couple of teachers talking about what a good kid he was. I wanted to meet him, so I found a way one day on the playground, simply striking up a conversation. I kept chipping away over the next several recesses and we soon became friends. He was already close with Rex Johnson; and in the sixth grade, by the time Tom Woolf had returned from South Carolina with a deep southern drawl, we were all best friends.

(Tom's father had gone there to become a plastic surgeon. I had no idea what that was until he stitched up my forehead with his new skills, when one of Rex "U-Haul" Johnson's front teeth left a gash there after a neighborhood game of touch football. Rex and I were about to tag Erv when he zigged right out from between us with the football. Erv was very elusive, it turned out. Remarkably, I didn't look any worse.)

Erv was innately handsome, maybe even a little rugged, with thick, wavy hair that he occasionally brushed out of his eyes. His family didn't have much money, so everything he had was his, truly his, including the sports car he bought with his earnings from various part-time jobs in high school. He was very athletic and, as noted above, probably should have been a running back on our high school football team. And, he was lucky. Lucky he didn't die on the side of a road in a Cambodian jungle in 2005 when he rolled his motorcycle and sustained life-threatening injuries. No one there would lend a hand, but a businessman from Chicago, traveling through the region, saw him and pulled over to help. Literally, he saved Erv's rapidly diminishing life that day.

The girls loved Erv, almost as much as they loved my other friend, Lew Bautista. Lew is the guy who inspired a room full of girls to squeal as he ran around the bases in third grade during a kickball game, all the way to home plate. We pleaded with the playground supervising teachers to remove them, but I think they enjoyed watching the spectacle. He was new to the school, transferring from who knows where. It was his first day of kickball and he couldn't come close to kicking that ball out of the infield. I usually got to third base or maybe all the way to home plate using my high top, laced up, logger boots to launch the ball out of the infield. But the girls didn't care about that. We waited to see who Lew would like before we offered to carry a girl's books home from school. Despite him stealing my girlfriend in the third grade, we also became best friends.

Erv's convertible MG Roadster was the dream car we all wanted. Not the turquoise Corvair I drove. Sitting reticently next to him in the cockpit as he attempted to get the engine to turn over, watching the dashboard shake as the rest of the car groaned and sputtered, I knew I was lucky, even though I always wondered if it would start or if we would be walking to the local mall to meet girls. By then he was dating some of the prettiest girls at our school. But Erv wasn't ready to settle down and get too serious. Instead, he went to college, studied history, and joined my fraternity a couple of years after I did. I think he did it for me and Rex (who also pledged that year).

He was extremely loyal, even though he never professed it. And honorable. I don't remember a time he ever disparaged anyone, even if others did. Erv, Rex, Lew and JR were there when I lost to Pat Roylance in my run to be fraternity president. We all went to dinner that night with some other close friends. They wanted to cheer me up. But I wasn't upset. I'd lost to a good man. A really good man.

Before Erv moved to Alaska and became a real estate developer, bush pilot and hunter of grizzly bears, he took me on a camping trip into the mountains that anchored one of our nearby hometown ski resorts. It was a pretty steep climb, with a promised hidden lake stocked full of cutthroat trout at the top of the mountain peak. On that day, however, he was still a rookie when it came to the great outdoors. (To be clear, I never graduated from rookie status.) We loaded up our backpacks with lots of nutritional things like canned soft drinks, pretzels and hotdogs; strapped on a tent, some sleeping bags and fishing gear, and headed up the mountain, leaving my car at the base near a stream, a detail that takes on new meaning later in my story.

The first thing I noticed was that our gear was incredibly heavy, causing us to move slowly, hand over hand. The second thing I noticed about halfway up the mountain was a flock of mosquitos hovering over my shoulder. They looked hungry. They were hungry. We were fodder. And we knew it. We didn't make it to the top that night. Neither did the mosquitos. They were patient, it turns out, feasting on us at their leisure. About 100 yards short of the peak at sunset, tired and hungry, with mosquito bites all over our extremities, we hurriedly put up the tent, rolled out our sleeping bags and walled ourselves off from the enemy. We ate chips and soft drinks and then dozed off.

Erv was up early the next day, loading his backpack and getting ready for the final ascent. I waved to him from my spot in the tent and wished him good luck. I said I would be hungry and ready to cook up some trout when he returned. He smiled and waved, feeling sorry for me, I'm sure. I watched him ascend until he was out of sight, grateful for an opportunity not to smile but to moan irreverently and curl up on the floor of the tent.

Erv returned unexpectedly. And empty handed. As we sat together on a log we had dragged into our camp area, he complained that the pond was empty. And, that other fishermen were already there when he arrived. Hard to believe. Where had they come from? As I gazed despairingly at the horizon I realized why. A trail of jeeps and four-wheel vehicles were traversing the far slope leading into the mountain's "secret" fishing hole. We could have driven to the top, or close to it, camped, fished, and ate everything in our backpacks, in time to return and look for girls in the city sans the mosquito bites. Erv's reaction when I pointed to the stream of vehicles was from the heart . . . and in typical fashion, colorfully expletive.

The story doesn't end there. It ends back at the stream that ran next to my car. Erv, on a whim, tossed in his line and caught several of those elusive cutthroat trout we had been looking for. We were best friends forever but that was our last camping trip together.

It was not our last trip together, however. I vividly remember taking a trip to the Pi Kappa Alpha national convention when I was later elected president of the house. I told him I was headed to Biloxi, Mississippi, where temperatures rivaled what you might experience in an indoor sauna room. "Never been to Biloxi," he said. "I'll come with you."

Two PIKE brothers picked us up at the airport. We didn't say much at all during the trip to our hotel. They did the talking. It was the first time I had ever seen racial prejudice and anger and even a kind of hatred boiling up in two human beings. Neither Erv nor I had good comebacks. I just knew

I wouldn't be coming to Biloxi again soon, and I was glad for that. I can't remember much else about the trip, except walking the streets of New Orleans, two single guys in their early twenties, listening to jazz groups and tasting more food on street corners and in restaurants than I would have ever thought possible. The mood that night was literally rocked by the appearance of a guy playing an electric guitar in the streets, with the longest cord I've ever seen, anchored to a speaker, following him around like a long snake. I'm not sure if the traditional Dixieland bands appreciated this raucous sound that was upstaging them. Not since the streets of Tijuana had I seen so much pandemonium. Remembering Tijuana probably helped us make the decision not to look for girls that night, especially to marry. Looking at Erv, though, I could tell he was relishing this. I saw adventure in his eyes. He wanted to stay up, walking the streets until dawn. I had meetings the next morning, and more Southern rhetoric to hear, potentially. So, I left him there alone and walked back to the hotel. He was more than fine with that.

Erv was stoic. Along with elusive. A wanderer of sorts. He didn't share too much. It wasn't until years later, as his life was ending, that I learned about the tragedy that engulfed him when he was five years old, and changed his world in a way that very few of us could ever understand. It shaped him and made him and drove him harder than he ever drove that MG sports coupe.

SEVEN

Rushing the Houses

I N THE SUMMER of 1965, when Erv, Tom and Rex were jumping out of military transports, I was being courted by college campus sanctioned fraternities. Fraternities began to appear as early as 1776 and history gives credit to a guy named John Heath, at the College of William and Mary, who started the first secret Greek fraternity, Phi Beta Kappa, after he was rejected by a couple of secret Latin societies. But it wasn't until 1825 that the first modern model of a Greek fraternity was started at Union College in New York. In 1851, the first sorority, called the Adelphean Society was formed at Wesleyan College in Macon, Georgia. Pi Kappa Alpha was founded on March 1, 1868 at the University of Virginia by six guys whose names I had to memorize and repeat over and over again during fraternity "Goat Week." I can only remember the name William Alexander, and I don't think he was the lead guy on this.

A batch of other fraternities were spawned around the same time in the Deep South, soon after the conclusion of the Civil War. They were (and still are I guess to some degree) elitist secret societies with strict codes of admission. The word "elitist" wasn't in my vocabulary when I joined a fraternity. But it's true that it only took one vote to "ding" you out of membership to any house during Rush Week. Of course, members were constantly negotiating for people they liked, and all you really needed was one respected ally to get through. I knew Tom Woolf's older brother, Bob. I admired him for his very suave and sincere demeanor. I was thinking he probably saw me as Tom's friend, and I wasn't sure if that was enough for him to pull for me. He probably remembered all the stupid things his younger brother's friends like me did, starting as young kids. We had a pretty good list when it came to being stupid.

Rush Week was stressful because you were never sure what people were saying about you behind closed doors (pledges weren't allowed in these meetings and had no vote). Active members had to pick and choose, and jostle a little, sort of like Congress does when it tries to put deals together to run the country. The Pi Kapps were probably a lot like Congress because they also had a political left wing and right wing, so to speak. I learned later that you had to be a little careful during these meetings, because if a right-wing guy dinged a left-wing rushee who was really wanted by one of his brothers, that brother might return the favor later, when a right-wing guy came up for vote. This jousting went on every night as meetings dragged on, sometimes until midnight or beyond. If you were an active member, you stayed, trying to protect and build the brotherhood the way you thought it should be, just like in Washington. This selection process goes way back to the time Greek fraternities took hold after the Civil War.

Freeman Hart, who authored *The History of Pi Kappa Alpha*, says this about the setting in Virginia at the time of its founding:

> "We see States and people who had a few years before been proud and assertive of their political rights now treated as conquered territory, disenfranchised and humiliated."

It's true that fraternities provided members with a sense of belonging and exclusivity. And self-esteem. Most of us want to be part of something, and in 1912, as the University of Utah campus grew, the Alpha Tau chapter of Pi Kappa Alpha was started by a bunch of guys with last names like Hatch, Callister, Brinton, Bagley, Hamilton, Dahlquist, and hilariously "one other member who has since been expelled."

Over time, membership grew, and by the mid '60s nearly a dozen fraternities and sororities bolstered hundreds of members at the university. Joining one of them was now prestigious, but they were still secretive. And white. Then Alpha Tau did something that led to it losing its chapter status in 1964. They pledged Denny Mia, the first Asian Pi Kapp. National HQ quickly disenfranchised them. Active members, headed by chapter president Jim Cannon along with the help of some alumni, got legal, and it wasn't long until the house was reinstated. On the trip back from the national headquarters in Virginia, Jim confessed that his room was next door to the legal team, and that he overheard them discussing the interrogation plan they were putting in place to discredit the "Utah boys." Unfortunately, the room's walls were thin enough that he was able to decipher their strategy and was well prepared for the next day. It was a story often told during Pi Kapp rush parties. The men were proud of their accomplishment. They even showcased Denny a little to make their point.

In late September of 1965, just as I was about to begin my life-changing History 101 class, Rush Week began. All summer, my friends and I had attended parties at frat houses or parks or in the backyards of nice homes that usually had a pool, a tennis court, a shuffleboard court, or maybe all of the above. We were courted by dozens of fraternity men who we met in whirlwind fashion, shaking hands and listening to stories about the virtues of each house. Towards the end of summer, we started being asked by our hosts which houses we were interested in. I loved at least three houses: Pi Kappa Alpha, Sigma Chi, and Beta Theta Pi. As I huddled with high school buddies Dave Boyce, Brent Eldredge, Kent Murdock, Keith Wallace, Craig Zwick and others, we began to speculate how we might end up in the same house. That is, if we were lucky enough to receive "bids" from the houses we were interested in. I began to sweat. I figured the girls from our school were sweating, too, as they felt the tension and pressure of being sorority hopefuls.

Rush Week started with everyone who wanted to join a fraternity visiting every house on campus. Door to door. There were close to a dozen active fraternities, along with the same number of sorority houses, within blocks of each other on Fraternity Row. To do that took all day and then some. It was very intimidating, looking at all these cool guys in argyle sweaters who were already members of a house. A few of them even smoked a pipe, which was very, very upperclassman-like. After spending twelve hours shaking hands and smiling at all these upperclassmen, I was exhausted and my hand ached from all the strong grips I kept receiving from some of my potential future brothers.

At the end of the day rushees turned in a preferred list of four to five houses to visit again. Fraternities and sororities did the same thing. All you could hope for was that your list somewhat matched their list. Mathematically, your chances were pretty good to have at least one match.

I had a wonderful high school experience, and a group of friends I was lucky to pal around with. But I didn't run for a student body office, play a sport, participate in the school band, or even be a member of the Chess Club. So I had no idea what my list would look like the next day. I don't think I slept that night, thinking about whether I would ever get a chance to be a brother in one of these houses. When all of the houses I requested invited me back the next day, I was taken aback. Maybe I wasn't so stupid or socially inept after all, I thought.

Things got tricky after that, because now it became sort of a game. Houses started having private parties for the rushees who had made the first cut, and sometimes two houses might have a party at the same time. One could be at one of the frat houses, and one might be out in the country at one of the member's parents' house. It was dicey trying to fit them all in. It was like having two dates on Saturday night, something I was never successful at pulling off, especially in my turquoise Corvair.

I soon learned that there were at least three houses I liked that seemed to like me back. By the end of September, I pledged Pi Kappa Alpha. The Pi Kapps had a wonderful reputation, even though some of the houses called them "the Army" because they were supposedly less discriminate about who they invited to join their ranks. The Pi Kapps said they were more interested in diversity. Diversity appealed to me.

Steve Anderson, Brent Eldredge, John Nelson, Ed Muir, Craig Zwick and I ended up Pi Kapps but our other friends dispersed to different houses. Dave Boyce and Kent Murdock went "Beta," and Keith Wallace joined the Sigma Chi house. During Rush Week I learned that Beta's were sometimes tagged as cool guys and sharp dressers, the Sigma Chi's were viewed as mostly former high school student body officers, Kappa Sig's and Sigma Nu's were partiers, and everyone else was a Pi Kapp. At least that was how some of the houses were being branded. I liked the Pi Kapps and chose them over the others, but just barely. Actually, it took me and a couple other guys a little longer to choose, and the Fraternity Board excused us for being late. House President Wally Boyack was especially patient and helpful while I was indecisive. In the end, I decided I felt more comfortable trying to become a Pi Kapp. I liked the idea of mingling with guys from the left and right side of the world. Later, I figured out that all of the houses were good houses, with good men and lots of diversity. Like IBM. Or Xerox for instance. Now I can't tell a Pi Kapp from a Sigma Chi, or a Beta Theta Pi or just about any other fraternity when I meet one of them on the street.

On a warm Sunday afternoon, with mostly red, yellow and orange leaves falling onto the ground all around the tree lined streets of the frat and sorority houses, the Pi Kapps held their traditional "Caravan," driving hundreds of young, winsome female pledges to their chosen sorority in convertibles. I scanned our parade of cars for the girl I would marry, but none of them seemed to pay attention to me. Mostly they squealed excitedly as we drove along Fraternity Row and dropped them off in front of their new homes.

EIGHT

Pledges

SUDDENLY RUSH WEEK was over, ending way too soon as far as I was concerned. I had loved being surrounded and catered to by others who seemed like they were almost begging me to join their fraternity. I liked all of the houses. I wanted to join them all. But I was no longer being courted by any of them. Now I was just a pledge at Pi Kappa Alpha. Stardom had vanished, just like that.

To pledge means to commit to something; it doesn't necessarily mean the reverse is true. Nothing was a sure thing until you suffered through "Goat Week," which didn't sound like a waltz-in-the-park kind of a week to me. Until that happened, I had "pledge duties," like cleaning up after lunch and dinner, sweeping the porch and front steps so the brothers could hang out there, and occasionally cleaning someone's room. The only thing worse than cleaning someone's room was serving dinner to the active members in the dining room. You could scrub someone's bedroom in private without getting harassed. But an "anything goes" attitude prevailed in the dining room as brothers sometimes tried to one-up each other, demeaning us pledges. Serving dinner could be intimidating; cleaning someone's room, tortuous (especially a couple of the more unkempt brothers' rooms). From my view, both experiences should probably have gotten you a free pass during Goat Week.

Knowing I wasn't special anymore, I settled into a routine. School, lunch at the house, a little more school, maybe some studying, and then some hanging out at the house. I and the rest of my 25 pledge brothers were all learning how to be fraternity men, trying to fit into a house with a bunch of guys we didn't really know, and who didn't appear to like us as much as they did just a little while ago. Especially at dinner. It took a little time to acclimate, but over time we all got to know our active brothers better. They were smart. Talented. And going places. I got to know Bob Woolf better too, who I suspected sponsored me during those grueling Rush Week meetings. Soon he would be headed to dental school to study orthodontics, and marry his very cute girlfriend, who we would imminently elect as our new "dream girl;" and whom would get "pinned" by him one night with all of us standing around a crowded living room in the Alpha Chi house.

I had to remind myself that I was in college. Getting a degree looked like an uphill fight. Especially with an average of 15 hours of classes each school term, with cute girls running all over campus and them not paying too much attention to me, either. Not to mention History 101.

Fraternity life took the edge off campus life. It was a refuge. We had weekly chapter meetings, and I became friends with my fellow plebes over lunches at the house, and during evenings hanging around playing pool, watching upperclassmen play poker, or spying a few brothers stumbling in after a night of studying or drinking. Or both. I looked forward to entering the more formal bonds of friendship with all 25 pledge brothers, none of whom had signed up for my TV class, History 101. I met

Pat Roylance who had attended a different local high school, and I became closer to high school friends Steve Anderson, John Nelson, Brent Eldredge and Craig Zwick, among others. Pat seemed to take me under his wing a little. I liked that. He was studying journalism, which I also liked. I loved his sense of humor, his confidence and his bravado. He had actually installed an old mattress in the back of his Volkswagen van so he could neck with girls in first-class fashion.

Even if Actives seemed a little distant or aloof, they noticed if you weren't around and let you know about it the next time you stopped by the house. You might even be encouraged to reach out to one of your pledge brothers if they had been MIA.

This is around the time when I first heard the term "sneak." Every pledge class was expected to have at least one before Goat Week. It meant kidnapping an active brother, stealing him away and then tying him up in some far-off public place in only his underwear. Or something like that. Of course, the idea behind this, which we didn't realize right away, was that once you pulled it off, all the other active brothers could start verbally abusing you in preparation for Goat Week, when it would be payback time. We didn't think that far ahead because sneaking someone, especially someone who often gave us pledges a hard time, sounded entertaining. Besides, our big brothers said it was a way for us to bond. To surprise us, the active members of the chapter actually "sneaked" one of our pledge brothers, John Nelson, making him wear a dress when they left him in the stadium parking lot of a rival university about 50 miles to the south of us. "Nellie" had to call his girlfriend to retrieve him, dress and all. Luckily, they were on pretty good terms.

So, we began to kick around some ideas of how to have the world's best sneak, and we came up with what we thought was a good one. Not as good as Rex "U-Haul" Johnson's sneak, which years later, would have won "best sneak in the history of the world" if there had ever been such an award. I think someone should have created the award and given it to Rex on national television. It was that good.

1965

Finding the Great Society

In 1965, the year I became a Pi Kapp, Lyndon Johnson was the President of the United States. He took over for his beloved predecessor John F. Kennedy back in November of 1963, following Kennedy's assassination by Lee Harvey Oswald. In January that year, during his State of the Union address, Johnson introduced the idea of the "Great Society," where the future would be bright for everyone. In May he was hanged in effigy after fifty college men at Berkeley burned their draft cards. *My Fair Lady* won the Academy Award for Best Picture. Malcom X was assassinated in Manhattan. The Beatles held history's first-ever outdoor stadium rock concert at Shea Stadium in New York City. About 3,500 soldiers were sent overseas to kick off the Vietnam War. Rodney King was born. At least 1,600 civil rights marchers walked through Birmingham, Alabama. A couple of months later, Martin Luther King led 3,200 demonstrators from Selma, Alabama to the capitol building in Montgomery. Sandy Koufax of the Dodgers pitched a perfect game against the Cubs in Chicago. Roger Allen LaPorte set himself on fire in front of the United Nations building to protest the Vietnam War. The Pentagon asked President Johnson to escalate the war by sending 400,000 troops to Vietnam. And, believe it or not, the first skateboard championships were held in Los Angeles. These are all things I didn't learn in US History 101 that year.

NINE

Dinner by RSVP Only

FUTURE BANK PRESIDENT and pledge brother Scott Anderson and I were assigned to serve dinner to the active house members on a rather cool October Monday night, not too long after Rush Week ended. It came as part of every pledge's duties. We had to bone up on things like placing the silverware in the correct position, and serving from the right side and retrieving from the left (or was it the other way around?), and we did everything but carry a nicely pressed cloth napkin over our arm during dinner. The house had a full-time cook who made lunch and dinner five days a week. We were living the high life, even as pledges. We could get a hot lunch every day for a small price, but dinner was only prepared for the active members who lived in the frat house. Our cook was adequate as I remember her, a little plump and short with a nice smile and a small fishnet over her brown, curly hairdo. Not every dish she prepared was overly appealing, especially when it was a hotdog casserole. But at least she was there. I wondered how she was able to endure hearing a bunch of 20-year-old guys talk about their collegiate exploits every day. She must have gotten fed up with us (no pun intended) because she left a couple years later. We never replaced her. She was a hard commodity to find. We still gathered in the dining room which could easily accommodate a bunch of us, but now we had to bring or make our own lunch, which required extra effort and reduced my studying time significantly.

Scott seemed like a serious student and a quiet gentleman, the kind any parents would naturally adore, but there was another side to him. The night of our assignment he smuggled in Ex-Lax, the over-the-counter laxative, which he had whipped up to look like chocolate frosting for the donuts he had purchased.

"You really think we should do this?" I said to him.

"Of course," he quipped. "Who will ever know it was us?"

However, the actives who lived in the house and had dinner that night were way ahead of us. Most of them knew very early on. And—using knowledge gained from philosophy classes, perhaps—they eliminated from suspicion the cook who got paid for her work, and deduced that it was probably the two smartass pledge brothers with the chocolate donuts who had caused the disturbances in their stomachs. This all happened pretty quickly, after they started comparing notes about how their digestive systems had been behaving since we served them dinner. In a fitting reprise, our "brothers" hosted us for our own "dinner" complete with "ash trays" as they called them (large buckets which became quite useful) as we ingested all kinds of foods I had never seen or heard of before. Or since. They made sure we suffered the results of their carefully concocted meal in record time. Evidently, it had once been the cuisine for a dinner during Goat Week, but had been retired before any charges of abuse could be filed by a disgruntled pledge. We finished dinner as soon as we could, thanks to continual prodding from the full-time residents of the house. The effects, however, lingered for hours. Ex-Lax was, by far, extremely inferior when it came to manipulating one's digestive system. It was a price we paid for our culinary contribution to the otherwise safe and relatively healthy dinners they were served most nights.

In the meantime, my pledge brothers and I began planning our own "sneak" of an active Pi Kapp. I was now committed to making sure I did my part to help make it supremely successful. Though far from being tasty, my Goat Dinner had been motivating. In more ways than one. I wanted to return the same kindness, even if only to just a single brother. With or without an ash tray.

TEN

PR Guy

HE HAD AN extensive vocabulary chock-full of words he used regularly to articulate his thoughts. He was tall and good-looking but not necessarily Rock Hudson handsome. He had a wonderful, slightly self-deprecating sense of humor. And an admirable IQ. Somehow Pat Roylance and I became friends. He had been a student body officer at East High School, which was down the street a ways from my school. We probably never would have met if we both hadn't joined Pi Kappa Alpha in the late summer of 1965, the year the Vietnam War escalated.

I don't remember much about his family except that his mother was very bright, too. And that his brother had joined Scientology. Pat told me his brother had to hold something that looked like a soup can in each hand with a wire from each one that connected into some kind of metered box. Based on the reading on the meter, you got in. Or not. Pat shook his head dejectedly when he told me his brother was in. I had never heard of Scientology and wouldn't again until Tom Cruise, and later Leah Remini, made it famous. In life I think we all look for validation, and Scientology was one way to get it. Fraternities were another, only better in my opinion. While I was trying to decide which fraternity to join, Pat, who I had just met, wrote me a letter telling me why he was choosing Pi Kappa Alpha, encouraging me to join him. I was touched.

Pat and I each had a favorite girl or two we dated. Pat's favorite was Marilyn Matheson, or "Matty" as she was known by most everyone. She was a beautiful girl, intelligent and thoughtful, and she usually carried an inviting smile around with her. Matty was a member of Alpha Chi sorority. I think she was the reason Pat took the mattress out of the back of his VW van. They would eventually get married, right about the time they graduated from the university.

As the year went on, and US History 101 neared its end, and the reality of the rapidly expanding Vietnam War and approaching military draft sunk in, John Nelson suggested that Pat, Steve "Andy" Anderson and I join the US Army Reserves. I liked the idea only slightly more than the Ex-Lax idea Scott Anderson had come up with a few months earlier. Pat said it would be a good way to avoid the "Saigon Scholarship" you might receive if your draft number wasn't high enough. So, we did it. John's dad was a recruiting officer for the Army, and in retrospect, he may have been a little behind in his quota that month. He told us if we didn't join immediately, we would miss out on Summer Camp in Southern California. What he didn't tell us was that it would be at Camp Roberts, just inside "Death Valley," California. It's called "Death Valley" for a reason. I never found out who this Roberts guy was they named the base after, but he had to have been a very lonely, unpopular man.

Before our experience in Death Valley, though, we started our regular training at Fort Douglas, which was right next to the university campus. This guy Douglas had to be more well-thought-of than Roberts, because the facilities there were nothing like the ones in Death Valley. They had trees, and buildings, and well-kept lawns, not sand and metal Quonset huts that captured most of the sunlight on the planet and turned the insides of the corrugated, aluminum-looking edifices into infernos. I'm not exaggerating. It could get as hot as 115 degrees in Death Valley even *without* the metal huts with bunks and toilets inside them. Luckily, they also had showers to go with the bunks and toilets. Cold showers. They came in handy.

At Fort Douglas we got to wear our green Army fatigues for two weekend days once a month for training. We had joined the 419th Armored Division of the US Army. Borge Anderson was our commander. The four of us received our Military Occupational Specialty (MOS) training assignments. We were to become advanced infantry scouts. We were supposed to drive small tanks ("track vehicles" as they were called), but I never did. Go figure. I was awarded some kind of certificate that said I was trained to operate them, even though I only peered inside one a few times during my six years of training. That wasn't Borge's fault, by the way. A whole bunch of things happened in the Army that kept me from doing more than just peering inside these mini-tank contraptions.

Weekends in the Army Reserves were long. Minutes seemed like hours, etc. Sometimes we managed to escape. The frat house was less than a mile away, and I thought I could learn as much sitting on those steps as roaming around an armory. Pat was pretty smooth at walking away nonchalantly from training. He slipped up one day, however, when our staff sergeant called his house. Pat answered. Not a good idea. The sergeant asked if this was Pat. Pat responded (another bad idea) with, "No, this is my brother." I said that Pat had a very high IQ, and he did. He just forgot about it for a second that day.

We soon realized that the Army was watching us more than

we thought. Over several weeks of meetings, I noticed that another guy named "Goff" (at least that was the name stitched across the front of his Army greens) was often near me and my buddies. One day, I asked him what his job was. He said, "I have several jobs in the Army, but one of them, quite frankly, is to keep an eye on you guys." You would think that might stop us cold in our tracks. But it didn't.

One morning we decided to skip some training sitting in track vehicles and go to breakfast at a well-known greasy spoon in midtown. It was called Bill and Nada's Cafe. It wasn't fancy but they served up a pretty tasty, high cholesterol breakfast. We figured no one would miss the four of us when there were already a couple hundred other Army guys wearing exactly the same stuff as we were, looking for something to do at the armory. Bill and Nada's would be off the grid for sure.

Turns out we miscalculated the appeal of Bill and Nada's. I hadn't even finished my first pancake when just inside the door I saw four soldiers. The first one was my captain. Right behind him stood his first sergeant. The captain is the head guy, but the first sergeant is the trigger man for the captain. He's the enforcer, and all first sergeants relish this as their life-calling. I can't remember his name but you could tell who he was by the big chevron with six stripes plastered on his left sleeve. It seemed to glow like a neon sign. Two other soldiers stood behind them, but it didn't matter who they were. We were busted.

In a wonderful twist of fate, however, they weren't looking for us. They were looking for a table at Bill and Nada's. What are the odds? So someone, probably Nada, ushered them passed our table on the way to theirs. Captain Anderson turned his head towards us and winked as they walked by. The first sergeant and the other guys didn't glance our way. In fact, they looked pretty stern and perhaps a little disappointed the captain was giving us a pass. What else could he do, though? After all, they had been busted too. They were probably a little bored and hungry for some extra calories, like us. We made sure we got back to the base before them. I always loved Captain Anderson. He was a tough military guy, but he knew when to let things ride. Especially at breakfast.

Experiences like the Army and the fraternity helped Pat, John, Andy and I create long-lasting friendships. I considered us equals even though Pat had that good IQ. Sitting on the front porch, these guys were always a welcome sight, especially as we began our illustrious college careers. Pat was a journalism student, and while he was in Washington, we exchanged letters quite often. I didn't consider myself an especially gifted writer, but it was fun trading stories and telling each other how much we were learning in our separate worlds.

Pat earned a degree, married Marilyn, and went to work for a congressman in Washington, D.C., doing public relations work. It seemed to me Pat ended his college career too soon. Part of that was probably because he found a great girl to marry who wanted to actually marry him, too. That was the problem with finding the girl you wanted to marry. It had to go both ways. Thanks to his being a pretty prolific journalist and correspondent, our friendship continued. In those pre-internet days you had to write paper letters, address them, stamp them, find a mailbox, and wait for a return letter.

Despite all that hassle, letters were fun to write and read. I told him about how my vertical leap in basketball was becoming less vertical. He told me about all his experiences at work and about all the fun he and Marilyn were having being married. I wasn't jealous. I was having a pretty good time hanging around the house, shooting hoops and attending some classes on a need-to basis. And, of course, looking for the right girl to marry, the girl that would be willing take me on, too. I was probably a bit of a project although I didn't realize it at the time.

Pat and I kept in touch almost weekly. I looked forward to hearing what he had to say about Washington DC, and how he was finding purpose in life. He and Matty had started a family by having two beautiful little girls, a couple years apart. He was happy. I wish I had held onto the letters because they were fun to read and full of Pat Roylance wisdom. He seemed to get wiser every day. Plus, he never lost his sense of humor. I liked all of his letters. Except one.

ELEVEN

Fishing Nets and Tennis Rackets

THE DAY WE decided to "sneak" an Active brother, tie him up, put him in the trunk of a car, and drive 75 miles north to exchange him for an Active Pi Kapp from Utah State University, we thought it might be a good idea to use a fishing net. He was a bit cantankerous to us pledges, so that's probably why we picked him. He was a big-time star for Utah's tennis team, too. We liked the idea of stealing a celebrity. Our plan was to surprise him during a practice at the local tennis club, even though we secretly thought it would be great to snatch him right in front of his opponent during a tennis match. But after weighing the different scenarios that could happen during his match, we opted for a practice. The fishing net—and it was a big, big net, almost like you'd see hanging over a tugboat—would be handy because we knew he wouldn't go easily, especially with the large, wooden tennis racket he would be swinging at us. I have no idea who found the fishing net. It might have come from the décor of a local fish restaurant that was in the family of one of our pledges, Mike Weilenmann.

Someone once said that the first twenty seconds in a battle are the toughest. And they were right. It took all 26 of us to surround him, get the fishing net over the top of his flailing body, drag him off the court, and then carry him like a heavy, squirming marlin out the door of the practice facility before anyone was able to rally for him. He fit nicely in the trunk of our car, however. And after a while, he stopped screaming as we drove, caravan style, to our destination. He did vow that none of us would ever survive Goat Week which was coming up on the near horizon. I think that idea started to stick in our minds, at least a little.

Even with that, we thought our sneak was pretty cool. All 26 of us had a big stake in Goat Week and would have to stick together when the hazing began. Of course, he didn't wait for Goat Week. He started hazing us as soon as he got back from being chained to a flagpole on Utah State's campus wearing just his skivvies. I didn't see what the big deal was about that. It was spring, not winter. It couldn't have been that cold. Maybe it was early spring, now that I think of it. Of course there's the fact that Utah State was usually ten degrees colder than our campus. And it was later in the evening, when the temperature probably drops another ten degrees or so. Maybe he had a point.

TWELVE

Goats

BACK WHEN I went through Goat Week, it was a far different affair than it is now. It actually started to change even then. We still received some "hazing" from our Active brothers, but they put away the paddles they used to spank you with, and they stopped doing other things like serving up a Goat Dinner, similar to the one my pledge brother Scott Anderson and I had tried to digest several months earlier. (They did make an exception in our case.)

Lance Parker, a genius-type philosopher who lived in the house, actually wrote a whole new Goat Week program called "Ingress." It was supposed to be a "kinder, gentler" Goat Week, to quote a phrase. Since I had nothing to compare it with, I wondered how good we really had it when I went through Ingress. We had to take ice cold showers and stay up late into the night, or get awakened in the middle of the night. No one talked to us unless they yelled at us to do some kind of chore. Or pushups. We did have discussion sessions at night, which I guess were supposed to unite us. I think what Lance did was groundbreaking even though it seemed like a tough week at the time. His program for our chapter, Alpha Tau, led to national headquarters making changes. The good thing is, no one got paddled, no one had to eat the famous Goat Dinner Scott Anderson and I had enjoyed, no one was forced to drink alcohol or really drink anything at all, and no one was ever threatened with a gun or was actually shot, like someone in a fraternity somewhere else in the country recently. We did have our best friend, who we had "sneaked" away some months before, breathing down our necks like a Marine drill sergeant. I have forgotten just about everything that happened that week, including even him harassing us.

I do remember feeling bummed out all week, walking around campus comatose, not being able to talk to my girlfriend because an Active member might see me, and trying to stay awake more than usual in classes. I was very relieved when it was all over, and I became an Active member of Alpha Tau chapter, Pi Kappa Alpha, number 1504 to be exact. I was tired of ice-cold showers. Even more than History 101.

Luckily, nothing serious ever happened to anyone in any of the Ingress Weeks that were held during my stint at the Pi Kapp house. There may have been a close call once, when during a ceremony with candles, an Active brother's ceremonial robe apparently caught fire. I'm sure the pledges going through that Goat Week thought that was okay, even though they probably didn't let on.

Later, when I was on the other side of Goat Week, I didn't get overly involved, harassing the pledge classes or making them shine my shoes or clean my room. Some guys really seemed to enjoy that, especially since they'd been victims before. Payback time had some rewards, evidently. I especially didn't like it when some of my good friends went through Ingress, like Lew, U-Haul Johnson and Erv. I was more of an observer, not a participant. I remember Erv, the free-spirited adventurer that he innately was, reacting almost like a caged animal at one point in the week. I think these ritual weeks of initiation have become a lot tamer these days. We live in a different world now. The word "abuse" shows up more frequently. It would probably make a top-ten list today as far as words are concerned. And for good reason. But that word didn't even show up when I went through Goat Week back in 1966.

THIRTEEN

Brothers in Arms

FRATERNITIES ARE BIG on brotherhood. I like the idea of brotherhood. And having brothers. I didn't have any growing up, just a sister I harassed incessantly. So, bonding with other guys who were more or less in the same boat appealed to me. Having a sister made me think it was less complicated being a guy. Less drama, for one thing. I found it pretty easy hanging out with guys, doing nothing, especially on the front porch of our fraternity house. I didn't see many girls hanging out on the front porch of a sorority house unless they were waiting for a guy to pick them up for a date. They were more discreet. More about doing. Guys seemed more about just being. We lived pretty uncomplicated lives. We weren't as good at keeping up appearances.

And, on the front porch, guys could come and go. It didn't matter who you hung with, and who stayed and didn't, because pretty soon another guy would come along and just hang out, replacing the guy who left, fitting right into the conversation.

I'm not saying guys always get along. Because we don't. In my experience, however, it seems to me that most guys are able to do nothing and be happy creating a little mischief. Once

I asked one of my sons, stumbling upon him and his friend in our backyard sandbox, "What are you guys doing?" His answer summed it up pretty well. He just looked over his shoulder and said, "Stuff." Turns out he and a couple of friends were blowing up toy action figures with firecrackers. I could see a fraternity front porch in his future.

As for me, I started thinking early that it would be important to have friends who could be close like brothers. Some of my best friendships started way back in elementary school and have continued ever since. Lew, Erv, Rex, JR and Steve Bushnell have always been close to me, separated only by miles, not so much by differences. My time with Pat, Andy, Glenn, Nellie, Hondo, Gold and Al Bluth were wonderful friendships that also developed during our college days together.

Pat and I became close probably because we both liked writing. That kept us connected years after he graduated and moved to Washington DC. In college, we were often together on the front steps of the frat house, or in the barracks of our Army Reserve unit, where pranks helped us keep sane. Nellie and Andy were wry dogs when it came to pranks in the Army. They could pull them off straight-faced while Pat and I often lost it, squelching our laughter and muffling our mouths with our hands while tears collected around the bottom of our eyes.

When it came time to go to basic training, Pat and I ended up being dispatched about a week apart to Fort Lewis, Washington. We weren't consistent churchgoers at the time, but suddenly church on Sunday seemed like a good idea. We met at church inside Fort Lewis and then Fort Knox every Sunday, trading stories about the previous week's exhausting drills.

I spoke with JR and Lew today, right after we had an earthquake nearby that registered 5.7 on the Richter scale, shaking bricks off buildings and causing me to run around purposelessly in my bedroom at 7:10 am while my wife tried to calm me down. Still good friends with these guys, I'm concerned about how each is doing. U-Haul Johnson, the recipient of somewhere around thirty neck and shoulder surgeries due to a progressive arthritic condition, stays in touch too. Steve Anderson and I became close too, living in the fraternity house together and occasionally in Army barracks in places like Death Valley. The Army made us payroll clerks for some reason, so we spent a lot of time paying our military brothers but never really seemed to get a lot of credit for it. John Nelson was the Chief of High Pranks in the frat house and the military. You never knew what he would come up with next. Glen Holley was my little brother in the fraternity. You're supposed to be sort of a mentor to your little brother, but I'm not sure if he saw me in that light. I can't talk to Erv anymore. Not directly anyway. Or Pat.

Even though I didn't have a real brother, I've been lucky to have a bunch of brothers, more than I recount here, that go way back. Many of those friendships were solidified in the house at 51 North Wolcott Street.

"Brothers-in-arms," by the way, is a phrase that started somewhere around 1480 AD, and refers to soldiers or comrades engaged in a common struggle. It wasn't life or death for most of us frat boys, but there was enough going on in the world around us that I don't feel bad referring to my Pi Kapp brothers this way.

FOURTEEN

Gimme Shelter

THE TITLE AND lyrics of maybe the best song the Rolling Stones ever wrote, "Gimme Shelter" epitomized what our country was going through in the mid-to-late '60s:

Oh, see the storm is threatening
My very life today
If I don't get some shelter, oh yeah, I'm gonna fade away

The '60s brought the kind of social upheaval that we had never experienced before. Finding ourselves, and finding shelter from the social changes that surrounded everyone, became themes. Maybe that's why fraternities and sororities really thrived during this time. For so many, they were a home away from home. A place to go and find support, friendship, and maybe a little inspiration too. The black cloud of Vietnam hung over the country, and many of us bought the government line that had started in the late '50s, that communism might sweep the world, especially if it got a foothold in Southeast Asia, which was where it could turn into a universal threat. Sixty thousand American soldiers would die and over 300,000 would be wounded, not to mention all the men and women who suffered from PTSD and other psychological injuries, including drug and alcohol addiction, in a war that certainly seems pointless today.

Where could you hide, especially with the military draft being put in place? Violence, racial injustice, and poverty were dividing our country. No end in sight. Frat life was my solace and comfort. There was danger out there in the world, lurking closer than I wanted it to be.

War, it's just a shot a way, it's just a shot away.
Rape, murder! it's just a shot away, it's just a shot away.
Love, sisters, it's just a kiss away, it's just a kiss away, kiss
away, kiss away.

The Rolling Stones

The other song that became an anthem for some during that time was Buffalo Springfield's foreboding "For What it's Worth:"

There's something happening here
What it is ain't exactly clear
There's a man with a gun over there
Telling me I got to beware
I think it's time we stop, children, what's that sound
Everybody look what's going down

There's battle lines being drawn
Nobody's right if everybody's wrong
Young people speaking their minds
Getting so much resistance from behind

What a field-day for the heat
A thousand people in the street
Singing songs and carrying signs
Mostly say, hooray for our side

Paranoia strikes deep
Into your life it will creep
It starts when you're always afraid
You step out of line, the man come and take you away
It's time we stop, hey, what's that sound
Everybody look what's going down

In 1966, as the Vietnam War was surging, people began turning more to drugs. They offered an escape. And there was a mysterious aura surrounding all kinds of emerging drugs. People who wouldn't normally think of trying drugs became curious. Some "experimented" with drugs, almost like a hobby. Timothy Leary helped out here a lot. What led Leary to become a household name was that he was a bright, well-educated and respected psychologist at the University of California, Berkeley, and then at Harvard, where he did a lot of talking. He said in so many words that taking drugs was not only okay, but a pretty good idea. Allen Ginsberg called him "a hero of American consciousness." Not a bad endorsement from a world-famous poet. Others, over time, were not so high on him, though, "high" being the operative word. Leary began getting attention when he wrote *The Psychedelic Experience* in 1964. Then came the phrase from a book that tore through our fragile cultural makeup: "Turn On, Tune In, Drop Out." He proclaimed that drugs were not only a way to feel good, but a way to get in touch with yourself, and actually get more out of life. That's my interpretation of what he said, anyway. Today, under controlled conditions, drugs can be used in Therapy to help relieve mental and physical pain. But that wasn't a practice then.

We all knew drugs were still a scary proposition. Serious drugs like LSD, sometimes called "acid," were almost unheard of when I was in high school. Smoking or drinking was about the only affordable vice. Until one of the prettiest girls in my junior class did some. Not only pretty, but popular, and sought after. Maybe the "hottest" girl in school. She moved to my town from somewhere in California. One of our senior student body officers started hanging around with her almost as soon as she arrived. But she disappeared sometime during the early part of the next year, when I was a senior. We didn't know why. We found out when she came back a few months later. She just wasn't the same. She had the same smile, and the same beautiful face, but her countenance was different. She didn't say much, and when she did, she just didn't seem to connect with people. There was a sort of vacancy in her eyes, like maybe she was somewhere else in her mind. It was one of the very saddest things I ever remember from high school. It's the first time I heard someone say "drug overdose." I didn't have any intention of ending up like that; alive, technically, but not really there. It's still depressing to think about. She had the world on a string. Until she didn't.

By the time I was in college, The Vietnam War had become a frequent headline, and more and more on everyone's mind. Even though you felt a loyalty to your country, you might wonder in the back of your mind what the government was really thinking when it started sending young men (like me) over there to most likely get killed.

Timothy Leary became more popular. President Lyndon B. Johnson, not so much. Leary couldn't have run for President, but he could sure talk a good line about living fully and escaping reality through drugs. Famous rock bands, like The

Moody Blues, mentioned him in hit songs. It was easy to see how people were getting swept up in this new movement. LSD became a drug I heard more about. It was probably what that striking young girl in my high school took. I think that drugs changed her life forever, and it could do the same to others, too. It was rumored that drugs were often made unscientifically, and that it wouldn't be impossible to get a dose that was twice as powerful as it was supposed to be. I knew good people who didn't seem worried about that, and who I guessed were playing around with it, and other drugs, willing to risk their lives for temporary euphoria.

The world as I had known it started to fracture into pieces. As the darkness of the war spread across America, the idea to "turn on, tune in, drop out" spilled out into society, and became more mainstream. Anti-war sentiment grew. Thousands of college-aged kids started to grow long hair, wear beaded necklaces and bell bottom pants, and talk about "making love, not war." They began moving to places like Haight-Ashbury in Volkswagen buses covered with bright "psychedelic" paint. Or maybe just to the local park to smoke marijuana or take LSD.

Some of the guys in the frat house were smoking marijuana, but I never heard of or saw anyone take serious Leary-advocated drugs. I'm sure we weren't immune. But no one I knew suffered brain damage other than what you might experience in History 101. Going to college cost money. So did joining a fraternity or sorority. There was an end game in mind, and it didn't include taking a road to nowhere.

Smoking dope was trending higher in social circles, but considered less dangerous than taking drugs. Getting high was a little like getting drunk, only illegal at the time. The difference between the two wasn't noticeable, except brothers who got high seemed relaxed and at ease. Docile, in fact. Drunk brothers could get a little sloppy, perhaps, and loud, sometimes slurring their words as they raised their voices. Maybe even a little obnoxious as they became less inhibited. Funny how that worked. Looking at it on paper, one might wonder if the law should have been reversed just based on the behavior of some of its users.

To many, the government seemed to be going about things the wrong way, and protestors were shouting back at them. Violence soon became something that didn't just happen in the jungles of Vietnam. Lyndon Jonson sent 3,500 soldiers there in 1965, but he would multiply that by a hundredfold very soon. Ironically, I don't think he liked doing it. During his State of the Union Address in January 1966, he said:

War is always the same. It is young men dying before the fullness of their promise. It is trying to kill a man that you do not know well enough to even hate. Therefore, to know war is to know that there is still madness in the world.

Johnson had to juxtapose the horror of war with what he and other American leaders thought was the need to root out communism. Or maybe control some of the territories in Southeast Asia. I wish that he would have listened to his speech a few more times before sending so many young men and women into harm's way.

————————— 1966 —————————

Year of the Miniskirt

In 1966, the year I became an Active member of Pi Kappa Alpha fraternity, over 500,000 troops ended up fighting the war in Vietnam; the mini-skirt became America's fashion statement; and NASA launched and then aborted Gemini 8 after a few hours in space. Neil Armstrong was one of the pilots. The TV series *Star Trek* began, and so did *Batman*. The Monkees became a pop phenomenon, but the Beatles and Rolling Stones dominated the music world. The Beach Boys released one of their last hits, "Good Vibrations." A new house cost just over $20,000. The average American made a whopping $7,400 per year. Inflation was 3% and the stock market closed out the year at 785. Somewhere around 200,000 people protested the Vietnam War worldwide, and support for the war dropped from 52% to 37% according to a Gallup poll. Heavyweight champion Muhammad Ali declared himself a conscientious objector, refusing to go to war. College students began applying for a draft deferment. Cigarette packs started carrying a health warning. Disposable diapers were invented. Adam Sandler was born. So was Mike Tyson. The Black Panthers were formed. Sadly, America experienced its first mass shooting when ex-Marine Charles Whitman killed 14 people and wounded 31 others from a tower at the University of Texas. Most were students. And, Richard Speck murdered eight nurses in Chicago. Other than the mini-skirt and *Star Trek*, it didn't seem like a very good year. Maybe we weren't going to become "The Great Society" President Johnson had promised.

FIFTEEN

Army Life

THE BIGGEST PROBLEM with life in the military is that it feels boring 90 percent of the time. Unfortunately, during the other 10 percent you can get killed. So, the Army drills things into your head to help prevent that from happening. And they keep drilling. Again. And again. Drilling is pretty much what they do. They even call it "drills" to let you know what they are doing. I felt the initial training we got was aimed at someone in grade school, so it was easy for me to get restless and stir up a little trouble. That's probably when the Army should have sent some of us home for a couple of hours on those long weekends.

But it's hard to send someone home from summer camp, and that's where we found enough time to upset our commanding officers. While at Summer Camp at Fort Irwin around 1967, the jeep my buddies and I were driving in the desert suffered a flat tire. (I still wonder how the four of us ended up in the same jeep.) At the motor pool, out there in the sand, with no trees whatsoever, and temperatures at 100 degrees (Ft. Irwin is next door to Death Valley), the sergeant in charge of the motor pool told us they didn't have tire changing equipment. He gave us an extra-long two-by-four and said to put it on the tire, and then drive over it so we could pop the tire out of the rim. Please take a moment to visualize what I just said. Now imagine two or three jeeps driving around in circles in the red dust in front of you, driving over these wooden planks. With no success. We stood watching and wondering what the Army was thinking. What if we really had been in a war situation?

That's when my military training kicked in. Recalling a military lesson on observation, I noticed the major's jeep as it drove smartly in front of us with his own driver, who looked a little full of himself as he drove by. In fact, they both looked that way. The major was the guy in charge of this whole thing called summer camp; I had never seen him before. His driver pulled up in front of a big tent and they both went in. I figured it must be an important tent because very few people were going in and no one was coming out. I pictured a great big vending machine filled with ice cold Coca-Cola products and other snacks inside, which might be why no one was leaving. I also noticed a very nice spare tire positioned on the back of his shiny green jeep. Just about any fifteen-year-old boy would have done what I did: switch out the tires. It didn't take very long to remove his tire full of air and replace it with our tire with absolutely no air in it, although there was a moment or two when I thought it would have been good to have had a class on rapidly switching out spare tires on jeeps.

From time to time, we watched the major's jeep to see if it functioned properly during the rest of our stint at Fort Irwin. That doesn't mean we would have 'fessed up if he got a flat. I figured the major could probably get another tire easily, and it might have even been his fault for not ordering his men to bring more tire-changing equipment. This would be instructional for him, and he probably would never forget to bring that stuff again. Our jeep came in very handy because, as we found out, if you looked like you were busy doing something or going somewhere, other guys in charge, like captains and first sergeants and even majors usually didn't bother you. They just assumed you knew what you're were doing and where you were going. We elevated the term "joy riding" to new heights that summer.

Nighttime presented a different problem. Since we weren't very far up the military chain of command, we slept on the desert floor in sleeping bags. Rows of sleeping bags. At night it got cold. So, it was important to zip up your bag and cower inside it. In the morning, no matter how snug you were the night before, sand was everywhere. Most of it ended up in my hair, eyes and teeth. Because, as I said, there were no trees anywhere to be seen. No green oasis to plop down on, only sand. The Army thought ahead on this, though, and positioned showers around the sleeping bag areas. Each of them had a nice wraparound curtain with a large stand topped with a barrel of water. To take a shower, you merely had to uncork the water and let it fall over you while you washed up. What the Army didn't consider was the wind factor. Maybe no one took the time to scout out the desert before we got there. Because the wind blows all the time. Day and night. It didn't matter if I was zipped up tight in my sleeping bag or standing inside the industrial sized shower curtain. Nature found a way to blow sand all over me anyway, circulating sand around and over and underneath the drums. We were like magnets for sand. So, the showers worked really well for about thirty seconds, and then they didn't. Before I could dry off, I had more sand on me than when I started. It was still worth it, though, letting that cold water wash over me as the desert sun beat down on everyone else. Still, I can only remember taking one or two showers out there in the Mojave Desert, and I didn't write home about it.

After a week or so of traipsing around in the desert, mostly in jeeps, or marching on dirt roads, or crawling around mounds of sand, looking for the pretend enemy with binoculars, summer camp finally ended. My frat brother Andy and I decided to celebrate our last night in the desert by heading into the central base where rumors said there was a movie theatre. Nellie and Pat wisely chose not to come with us. Getting into town was a breeze. We just hitch-hiked our way into the base since it seemed like most of the tanks and vehicles were headed that way, probably to celebrate.

I daydreamed about the movie we might see when we arrived. I decided any chick flick, love story, comedy or even a drama would be wonderful. I guess some smart military guy thought a bunch of guys would rather not watch any of those movies after spending time together in the desert. Instead, he chose, unbelievably, *The Dirty Dozen*, a war story with Lee Marvin and a bunch of other guys. So, for a couple of hours we watched these Army heroes crawling around in the dirt, throwing grenades, and driving trucks and tanks all over Germany, I guess trying to rescue someone or blow stuff up.

Here's where it gets messy: After the movie, around 10 pm, we began looking for a ride back to camp, about 5 miles away. But the main road leading back into the desert was empty. No trucks. No tanks. *Why*, we wondered? About this time, we started to worry that we might have been missed by the major or some other guys. If they were looking for us and got mad, it might have been worth it knowing we had seen *Fantastic Voyage* with Raquel Welch in a skin-tight jumpsuit; *A Funny Thing Happened on the Way to the Forum* with Zero Mostel; *The Graduate* with Dustin Hoffman, Katherine Ross and Anne Bancroft; or even *Born Free*, the cute family movie about a girl and a lion. Sure, *The Dirty Dozen* was a pretty good movie, unless you were watching it in the middle of desert maneuvers with other guys dressed up just like you. I guarantee not one guy watching that movie had been daydreaming about tossing grenades or shooting up the enemy that day. They were probably dreaming about Raquel Welch, like me.

About an hour later, after walking much of the way, and occasionally getting a ride from a wayward jeep (it turns out all the equipment was supposed to be turned in by 9 pm, about an hour before the movie ended), we crept back into camp, practiced the low crawl like we had been taught all week, and stealthily shimmied into our sleeping bags. About thirty seconds later, before we could even snuggle in and zip up, we were standing at attention. Our commander, all bleary eyed, stood right in front of us. I mean *right* in front of us. He had been waiting with a long stick of some kind which he ratcheted across our sleeping bags. He was not happy.

Unfortunately, the whole unit had been rousted out of bed every half hour to hear their names for roll call because two idiots had gone somewhere, maybe into town to see Raquel Welch, and were now AWOL.

We tried to make up for it the next day by busily loading as much equipment onto the buses as we could. Even Pat and Nellie didn't seem too happy with us. Luckily, we had 'fessed up when the commander started dressing us down the night before. "No excuse, sir," was all we said about twenty times, in answer to all his questions. He told us later that until we did that, he had been thinking about a court martial, a term you really don't like to hear in the Army. I never watched *The Dirty Dozen* again.

You're probably thinking by now, *What a couple of screw-offs.* I realized we had pushed the limit, and that we had been pretty selfish, even if Raquel Welch or Katherine Ross had been waiting for us in town. I tried to be a little better after that.

Later, the war got worse. More men were dying in Vietnam.

It felt like we were losing the war and that the Viet Cong had outsmarted us, tempting us to fight a war in their jungles instead of somewhere else. They were sneaky. They knew how to fight in the jungle. We never figured out how to do it without suffering a lot. I think people, especially my age, started using drugs more, and protesting more. People just weren't happy about going to war. Especially a war it didn't look like we could win, and a war that looked more and more like it wouldn't accomplish anything good for our country. In 1968, the college student deferment ended, and on December 1, 1969, the US government conducted its first official draft for the war. It was a very emotional time.

Along with my frat buddies Pat, Andy and Nellie, who had all joined the Army Reserves at the same time, I didn't worry about the draft anymore since I was already serving. So, we hung around the fraternity house that night as some guys in Washington started randomly drawing little blue balls out of a big rotating bin. Each ball contained a date inside, representing someone's birthday. A bunch of our frat brothers were there, hovering around the TV in the living room. Watching and waiting. The first ball, assigned number, 001, was for the first guys who would be drafted and most assuredly sent to Vietnam, possibly to die. It was September 14. All the eligible-aged guys in America with that birthdate would soon be reporting for active duty in the military. I was born on September 24, or number 195 in the "draft lottery" if I hadn't already joined the Reserves. I thought if I went to Vietnam, I probably wouldn't come back. It seemed like it didn't matter how good you were, or how fast, or how strong, or how well you could shoot; if you were walking along a path in the jungle with your squadron, it pretty much came down to luck whether you would make it through without being picked off by an enemy soldier hiding in the bushes, or maybe a tree.

A friend of mine, who grew up in my neighborhood alongside me, went to Vietnam to fight. His name was Jim. When he came back on leave for a couple of weeks or so, I ran into him. I asked him what it was like. He wouldn't say anything, really. He just said that he would do anything not to go back. In fact, he said he wasn't going back. A few days later he died in an automobile accident, rolling his car off a steep embankment while driving on one of our canyon roads. He was alone. Another high school classmate joined the Marines to fight for our country, but became so disillusioned with the war that he gave all his military gear away and showed up for an inspection in just his military underwear. After spending six months in the brig, he died in a gun battle. Just before that happened, he sent his wife a letter, entitled "In Case I Die."

Thus, December 1, 1969 was not a particularly fun night at the frat house, even though quite a few of our brothers got drunk or high while they waited to hear the news. Scott Rushforth, who was one of those really brilliant-type frat guys, woke me up in my bedroom in the middle of the night. I was sleeping on the top bunk when he began shaking my bed, frantically asking me, "What's my number? I forgot my number!" Of course, there were at least fifty guys in the frat house that night, and I couldn't remember any numbers except mine, number 195, thinking I probably didn't need to have joined the Army Reserves.

SIXTEEN

110% Knight

WHEN I WAS Rush Chairman for the fraternity, I found JR Knight on a cold call from a list of freshmen living in the dorms. Fellow frat brother Tom Buxton recognized his name and recommended I give him a call. JR had a football scholarship he would make the most of. Once we became friends, he used to have me throw a football at him as hard as I could from about ten yards away, aiming for any part of his body, or anywhere within a couple feet of him. He wasn't particularly tall or especially fast, but he became a go-to wide receiver whenever the team needed ten yards, knowing he would catch anything even close to him. The other wide receiver was named "Speedy" Thomas, which is probably why JR had me notch those footballs I tossed at him anywhere but where he was expecting them. Looking back on it, maybe he picked me more for my lack of accuracy than my throwing arm.

JR became a consummate frat man. Now he was able to rub shoulders with someone besides the mostly freshman who resided in the dorms, where he began his college career. I pictured the dorms more like a hospital ward than a hotel or a study hall. When you are in a hospital ward recovering from surgery or a heart attack, all you can hear all night long are other patients recovering from surgeries and heart attacks moaning and talking in their sleep. The dorms must have been like that, only with fifty to a hundred guys running around in towels, yelling and boasting to their dormmates in the halls before they took to their beds to talk and moan in their sleep. JR went from that to what might look like the raucous environment at the frat house. But instead of maybe a hundred young men, only about twenty lived in the house, mostly juniors and seniors; and believe it or not, they were often studying to get into law school or medical school, or maybe just looking for some time on the front steps. It was a far different scene, because most of the dorms were packed with freshmen from out of town who thought they had four years of school ahead of them, more than enough time to make up for a little partying during their first year. JR seemed to mostly grin around the house after that. And he should have. We saved his butt, after all.

His full name was James Rodney Knight, and he got his middle name from his dad, Rod Knight, who had been a big-time athlete years earlier. Rod raised his family in Reno, Nevada, not too far from Battle Mountain, where JR met his future frat brother Charlie Seldin. They played against each other competitively in sports. Life was faster paced in Reno, not because it was bigger, but because it was . . . well, just faster. There were casinos and hotels equipped with all kinds of gambling tables because it was legal in Reno. So was prostitution. Rod owned a casino, so JR was familiar with that lifestyle, even though he was never interested in it. He was interested in becoming athlete of the year and student body president of his high school so he could leave Reno. When he joined the fraternity, I didn't think about how lonely he probably was in the dorms with his family a plane ride away.

He didn't talk much about family or brag about his father's athletic career. I know he loved and missed them. At one point he disappeared for a week or so. His mother had passed away, and he went home to be with his family. He didn't even bring it up when he returned. I worried about him a little, but he had a whole slug of brothers around to lift him up.

JR was a good student, and he especially loved business classes. I can't say I loved business classes, but I took them so I might have a little credibility when I started interviewing for jobs. Of course, I hadn't looked down the road far enough to see if there were any job interviews in my future yet. One of JR's finest attributes was that he was humble. He was always interested in how others were doing, and how he might be the best fraternity man he could be. I thought that talent would come in handy when he got married and raised a family.

During college JR and a couple of other buddies started a business designing and selling desk calendars to businesses around town. Years later, as a very successful businessman, he kept telling me about the importance of personal "cash flow" until one day, about the time I was going to retire, I realized what he meant all those years earlier. I was slow to figure some things out, as you probably know by now.

SEVENTEEN

Nicknames Tell a Story

IN FRATERNITIES, LOTS of the members are given nicknames. They can be quite endearing, but not always. For example, you might not appreciate being called Asphalt, if that was the name that stuck with you through college. I'm not sure how Jeff Jenkins got that name. Possibly because he may have been indiscriminate about where he laid down when he was a little inebriated; or perhaps as a big lefty pitcher for the university, it was where he occasionally threw a wild pitch. No matter how it originated, it wasn't so much a name you'd mark down on the endearing side of a ledger, if you were making a list. Jeff was a good natured, affable kid who was well thought of around the house. He had talent. The name didn't fit the man. But Asphalt wore it well. Without ire.

Lots of our frat brothers received an abbreviation of their given name. Like "Nellie" for John Nelson, "Goldie" for Brent Gold, "Nordy" for John Nordquist, and "Lewba" for Lew Bautista (although we also called him "Buddha" for his smile that looked just like the one on those carved Buddha dolls).

But many nicknames had a backstory associated with them. Jon Lervig was given the name "Heat" since he could throw a baseball about 100 mph. Scott Welling was a huge Boston

Celtics fan, and Greg Maxwell called him "Hondo" because that was the nickname the Celtics gave John Havlicek, his favorite player. Supposedly Havlicek looked like John Wayne in the old classic western movie *Hondo*. I'm sure some of our younger brothers couldn't remember his real name. Hondo turned into an attorney, not a cowboy or a basketball star. Greg Maxwell's nickname was "Nozzle," by the way, because his nose was positioned prominently on his face.

Steve Anderson, who stood around with me in the Army Reserves, was naturally called "Andy," but earned his real nickname "C-Note" on the card table in the back of the frat house because of his propensity to place $100 bets. Most of us didn't have $100 bills then, and I'm not sure C-Note did either. One of our brothers was called "Dirt Man," which is on the not-so-endearing side of the ledger. It wasn't a hygiene issue, as far as I could tell.

Al Bluth was nicknamed "Bwana." Like Buddha, he was one of the most handsome guys in the house; and with his perfectly combed black hair, he looked like he could be on vacation somewhere in the Caribbean. He sauntered as he walked, too, and liked Hawaiian shirts after spending a couple of years on the islands. Steve Keller, also a face man, had piercing blue eyes and got the name "Beede" for them.

Craig Boorman became "WOAPL," or "Worst Of All Possible Links," after being on a PIKE bowling team and so christened by the team captain, Norm Anderson. That wasn't on the endearing side of the list, either . . . but that didn't matter because most of us forgot what the name stood for anyway. Plus, Boorman was a genius, an excellent athlete, and a really good guy to boot.

From another era, there was "Fat Load," who probably patronized Snappy's Burgers more than I did. You probably didn't want to mess with Fat Load. I wonder if anyone called him that to his face. Others of note from previous times include: "Tex", "Jamba Juice," Erik "Nuts" Dewitz, and one of my personal favs, "Serta." I hope Serta graduated.

The house even had a "Flounder"—at least it wasn't "Guppy"—and "Llama," who would probably have been everyone's best friend. And then there was Danny "Flipper" Schoenfield and Nick "Cadillac" Powell.

John Nicolaysen will always be known as "Pizza" according to one of his brothers. I'm guessing he could have comfortably hung out with "Jamba Juice" and "Fat Load." Still in the food category, there was "Hot Dog" and "Sloppy Joe," and "Blu-Berry," the name given to Kevin Fitzpatrick, who earned it somehow in a drinking fest. He mostly went by Fitz, but a slightly inebriated sorority girl he met couldn't get it right, and kept calling him "Fritz," which outlasted everything else he had been called. Joe Busterud got the name "Rubba"—short for Rub-a-Dub, again due to a young woman not adept at pronunciation, at least at that particular moment. Joe Ribotto was the sports editor at the university newspaper and was christened "Scoop" by his frat bros.

In my day, Scott Storrs somehow earned the nickname "Stuntman," but I never saw him do even one backflip. Ralph Bates was called "Doc" because he was suave. Bob Clark, for some reason, was called "Booby." JR Knight was often called "110% Knight" because he was so competitive; he would call you out if you weren't giving, in his opinion, 110%. I had to tell him one day that one of the brothers he was chastising on the basketball court was indeed giving 110% and maybe more. Somebody went so far as to scratch "110%" into the door on his frat house room. In red, I think. JR was highly regarded at the house, so you paid attention to him if you were dogging it a little.

What fraternity would be complete without a "Fast Eddie"?

We had our version, Rich Edwards, and he really deserves his own chapter. But I am giving him his own paragraph. I didn't think Fast Eddie was going to do much more than take up a little space and drink religiously when I first met him. But I was wrong. Appearances are funny, because they're just that. What appears on the surface might not be what's really going on underneath, which is what makes up the real person. Now a retired skycap for a major airline, Fast Eddie became legendary for how well he took care of people coming and going from airports. Everyone knew Fast Eddie. When people arrived to catch a plane, he was the first guy they asked for. People would go out of their way to find him. People like pro golfers Mike Weir, Billy Casper, and Tony Finau. And music star, Marie Osmond. Just for starters. Whenever I traveled, I relied on Fast Eddie, too. I'm sure I got the same treatment as they did. Richard Edwards was just that way. He turned a good job into something special. He was the ultimate concierge. Today, Fast Eddie heads up several charities and has made a real difference in the lives of the people all around him.

Rich "Iron Man" Irion and Paul "Marco Polo" Markosian had nicknames that were ready-made for them. Don't know how Brent Eldredge picked up the name "Kiwi," but it stuck. Another brother who left his mark on the fraternity was Charlie "Bus" Seldin, who came all the way from Battle Mountain, Nevada to be a Pi Kapp, I'm assuming by Greyhound.

Some other notable names throughout Pi Kapp history include:

Rocko	Slash	Spanky
The Captain	Shorty	Slick
Train	Big Daddy	Cowboy
The Pillar of Morality	Nips	Radar
AJ Gravity	Pepper	Turbo

One of my personal favorite nicknames is "Duraflame." I never met him, but there has to be a good backstory there somewhere. Probably something to do with a chemistry experiment gone bad. Brandon Osborne got the name "Hagen" due to a misprint in a campus newsletter. One of the brothers I looked up to, a year or so older, was called "Froggy." Wouldn't be my first choice; but he, being a very jovial guy, made the most of it. Everyone liked Froggy. Years later, one Pi Kapp was nicknamed "Jill" because his best friend was named Jack. And believe it or not, there was actually a young man walking around the frat house with the nickname "Wednesday," for some reason.

Looking back, most of us probably didn't mind shedding our collegiate nomenclatures. You knew there was a story behind just about every name. Maybe not a good story, but there was invariably some humorous or perhaps incendiary event that followed a brother around for most of his college career, and maybe beyond.

My nickname was "Spike," and I have no idea how it was derived. It was given to me one day during an outdoor pickup basketball game by the guy who most aptly earned his own nickname, Rex "U-Haul" Johnson. I can't remember who first tagged Rex as U-Haul. I hope it was me. It was an easy call. He more than deserved it. He would soon become legendary.

EIGHTEEN

U-Haul Johnson

MY BUDDY FROM high school, who jumped out of airplanes for the Special Forces, and joined our fraternity when he was a junior with just four other pledges in the dead of winter, arrived just in time to register for some classes at the university. He had gone through Rush Week the previous quarter, but didn't receive a bid from our house. Later, Erv, Andy, Walt and I visited him at his home. His father had died and we told him he needed to be a Pi Kapp because he was floundering. He said he didn't have enough money to pay dues. Andy countered by telling him he could become the house manager, working for the house residents, and thus we could waive his dues. As house manager, he may have encouraged our cook to leave, sensing we might have had enough hotdog casseroles for a while. My guess is that she was more than ready to leave. Rex took up preparing lunches for the brothers. That didn't last too long, though.

Rex Johnson was extremely unpredictable, in many ways. Half the time I couldn't tell if he was my best friend or just mocking me behind his wry grin and glimmering eyes. His somewhat edgy behavior had probably intimidated or worried a few Active brothers when he had rushed the first time. He had some tall tales, too. Most of them probably happened in one way or another, maybe with a few modifications. The way he earned his nickname took ingenuity, and he had to deadpan his way through a month or maybe two in order to earn it. That's how long it took him to pull off the greatest sneak in frat history.

Rex grew up in a small home with just one brother. His dad drove a tanker truck on long road trips much of the time. He was a Teamster, professing his undying loyalty to Jimmy Hoffa whenever a conversation allowed. I remember his mom as having a husky voice that almost overpowered her small, attractive demeanor. She kept things together by working nights as a nurse so she could be home during the day to keep an eye on Rex. I could tell how much she loved Rex whenever I was at his house. His dad did, too. Since Rex was the oldest of two boys, he probably took the brunt of his parent's somewhat intransigent approach to parenting. Maybe there was good reason for that.

Like most of us, he liked hanging out and sleepovers with friends whenever he could get them. He was bright but mostly applied his innate intelligence to survival at home, and then parlayed that training into some degree of rebelliousness on the streets. When Tom Woolf and Erv Terry brought Rex into our small inner circle of high school friends, I wondered why. But I misjudged him, like some of the brothers in our fraternity house had during his first attempt to join. Over the years he has proven to be everything a friend could be, and more. When I was president of the fraternity, Rex was secretary (Incidentally, C-Note was treasurer), and I remember re-counting the votes for our dream girl with him in my room because only one vote separated the two finalists. Rex was a little unpredictable, which was part of his charm, but he was always there when you needed him. And always committed to making things right at the end of the day.

He worked at the local golf course with me, often at night, watering fairways and greens until almost dawn. I worked mostly the day shift. One night I backed my dad's huge Oldsmobile over a stake, angled and embedded in the cement in a vacant parking lot, puncturing his gas tank which quickly emptied out onto the ground. My date and I watched in awe as the gas gauge fell to empty in only a matter of seconds. I had wanted to impress my date, so that's why I had taken my dad's car instead of my turquoise Corvair with the engine in the back. I think the Olds had fins. Once it became impaled on the metal sheath that some idiot had left sticking out of the ground smack-dab in the middle of this vacant lot, just waiting for an Oldsmobile with fins on it, any chance of impressing my date evaporated, just like the gas that used to be in my dad's tank. I called Rex. He left work and brought me his little foreign car, a Renault, which I didn't think was a step up from my turquoise Corvair. After I dropped my date off, thinking I'd probably never see her again, I struggled to find reverse in his five-speed, grinding the gears in her driveway for a minute or two as a final tribute to the evening.

Not particularly interested in high fashion, Rex still looked stylish and composed. Girls liked him, although only a few could match his sarcastic humor. He loved golf and got pretty good at it. Like me, he understood basic things like a golf swing or a jump shot better than the dynamics of physics, chemistry or the Socratic Oath. We got along. As a twentysomething pledge, he had a leg up on the other pledges as well as some of the Actives. His mind was always in motion, and he seemed to have a plan for how to elevate a party to the next level; or conversely, to subdue it in a proportionate way, sometimes sitting alone with a few of the brothers after it ended prematurely. He could be the life of the party, or the death of it. It just depended on how the day went. Usually, though, he reveled in it being all that it could be. I really only remember one time, when we had invited the Alpha Chi sorority over for a barbecue out by the eight-foot-high basketball hoop in our backyard, that he put a damper on things by taking a leak, along with a brother from Sigma Chi, off the roof of the frat house into someone's new convertible Volkswagen coupe. Party over.

He was a good pledge, though. Likeable. Easy-going. And yet unpredictability was always in play. The active brothers never really expected his pledge class to sneak even one guy because it was so small. Most people joined fraternities in the fall, when school officially started, not in the dead of winter. People wondered, *what had these guys been doing with themselves in the fall, when they should have been in school?* Most of us didn't really know these new pledges and had zero expectations they would plan a sneak. After all, it had taken 26 guys in my pledge class to sneak one Active. Four against 70 or more active members weren't good odds. We never even considered the idea that he might single-handedly sneak about 30 Actives in one fell swoop in broad daylight. But that's what he did. As I said, his mind was always in motion. He was making plans. Not one of us was truly safe. Not even me, one of his supposed best friends.

NINETEEN

The Sneak, Part I

O NE DAY REX wrote these words on the large blackboard
anchored to the wall just inside the foyer of the Pi Kapp
house: "Peach Days—Coming Soon." When brothers
started asking what Peach Days was, Rex told them that he
and the other pledges were going to host a party in honor of
the Actives, named for an exotic dancer. "Peaches" was how
she was known by others, evidently. And, he had procured
her services for a yet-to-be-determined date, if some of the
brothers would be interested in helping foot the bill. Peaches
was popular, so there would be a bit of a financial obligation,
but not much when the cost could be spread around.

In the days that followed, as interest grew, more details
began to take shape. Peaches might be the centerpiece, but there
would be other things going on at the party. Cards, drinking,
maybe a little food. Brotherhood, in other words. Suddenly,
Rex went from being relatively unknown to a very popular guy.
People wanted to be part of Peach Days one way or another.
They started chipping in some money. No one knew what Rex
was doing with the money, but they trusted him. He seemed
really sincere. To everyone. I was amused but certainly not
suspicious.

Sneaks have been a thing in fraternity lore for years. Most pledge classes, especially those with larger numbers, did them. I remember C-Note Anderson jumping out of the staircase window next to the front door of the Pi Kapp house to escape some pledges' outreached hands.

Pledges have plotted all kinds of ways to capture Actives and make them disappear for a day or two. They've handcuffed them, tied them up with ropes, or even thrown a fishing net over them to contain them, like we did. They put them in attics, or basements, or chained them to flagpoles in public places without much clothing, like we did. Since my state hasn't made gambling legal, dropping someone off in Las Vegas or Evanston, Wyoming had a side benefit for pledges, and thus became popular destinations. One pledge class, in what I thought was an expeditious albeit expensive sneak, bought an airline ticket and sent an Active to Denver. A persuasive fellow, he was able to convince a woman he met at the airport to buy him lunch and a plane ticket home. When Rich Gibson was taken to the far end of the state, subsequent sneaks were called "Gibsons" for a while. One brother known as "Pizza" was sneaked to the far north part of the state and dropped off at the Pi Kapp house at another university. He thanked the brothers when they pushed him out of the car and spent a few extra days partying with the guys living in the frat house there. Sneaks didn't always go according to plan.

I suspect sneaks aren't very easy to pull off in the world we live in now. They might even border on being called abusive, like a lot of other things that we used to think were okay. But back in my era things were a little different, and Rex (soon to be "U-Haul Johnson") had a plan, a plan that would never be duplicated in the history of fraternity "sneaks"—and no one else knew about it.

TWENTY

The Perfect Frat Man

CHARLIE "BUS" SELDIN just might have been the perfect guy to fit into a fraternity. Second nature you might say. Stylish in a carefree way. Intelligent, but not academically oriented so much he couldn't enjoy frat life. Cool and calm. Witty to the point of sarcasm; he could do you in quickly if you decided to trade pithy comments with him. Handsome. Aloof. Girls liked him right off. Before I joined and learned about the depth and character of all my fraternity brothers, Bus would have been how I envisioned a typical fraternity man.

Charlie smoked a pipe and wore cardigan sweaters, but almost in protest. He wasn't trying to look cool. He just was. That's what probably got the attention of Robin Warburton, a beautiful 10-rated sorority girl he eventually married and with whom he raised two children. Of course, there was much more to Charlie, and Robin knew that early on, when they first started dating. They never dated anyone else again.

The only other girl in Charlie's life at the time was Sophie, the Saint Bernard, who was just slim enough to fit in the front door of the frat house. Sophie, the perfect definition of a frat house mascot, was a jovial canine who could almost leap into your arms, or at least put her paws on your shoulders when she wanted a little attention, or a sandwich, like the one she snatched away from one of our unsuspecting fraternity brothers, complete with logoed wax paper from a popular fast-food chain encircling it. That brother should have known, like most of the rest of us, that Sophie usually got what she wanted, and that it was good to pay attention when she was in the area. She devoured the sandwich in one gulp.

A natural athlete who grew up in Battle Mountain, Nevada, Bus had been competing against JR "110%" Knight in sports starting around the time he was twelve, continuing all the way to college. I first saw Charlie at a pick-up basketball game we had organized as a Rush party for prospective pledges. He shot lights out that day. He had my vote.

I don't know how he got the nickname "Bus," but I think he brought it with him to the Pi Kapp house, or else he earned it in some manner right after arriving. That's how I've always known him. Bus. Always on the move.

One memory I have of Charlie Seldin is of him sitting on the stairs just inside the front door of the frat house late one Saturday morning. Sophie was nearby. One of his fellow PIKEs was complaining to him. It seems he had lined Charlie up with one of his girlfriend's best friends the night before, and the date hadn't gone well. I think Charlie may have become slightly inebriated early on. Left his date. Wandered away. Mingled with others. Didn't remember taking her home, or if he even did. When our Pi Kapp brother had finished reminding him of all the extra effort that had gone into lining him up, and had berated Charlie for everything he didn't do to help his blind date enjoy the evening, Charlie had a very simple response. "Did she have a good time?" was all that rolled off his slightly hungover tongue.

Naturally, there were others who seemed like they were carved out for fraternity life, but with a more serious nature. Frat brothers we held up high, who were focused and dedicated to making things happen when school was behind them. Not that Bus or the rest of us weren't. Brian Swinton, who was Rush chairman in 1965 when I joined the fraternity, was articulate, impressive on all fronts, and a gentleman. He aspired to do great things, and he did, becoming a key executive at the Marriott Corporation. He took an interest in me and others and tucked us under his wing, so to speak. I think he helped groom me to be Rush chairman when he was house president. I couldn't have had a better internship anywhere on campus.

Many others at our Alpha Tau chapter exuded the same air of confidence and dedication, excelled at just about everything they did, and kept reminding us in very subtle ways that we would all have to grow up some day and take up some space in society. Some of us just weren't in a big hurry at the moment. Not while Sophie the Saint Bernard or Charlie, the perfect definition of a frat man, was around to entertain us. Luckily, Brian Swinton and a host of others were close by to keep us pointed in the right direction.

P.S., Charlie, a very creative fellow, went on to have a stellar career as an advertising executive. And he found time to work for a non-profit company, too. So there.

TWENTY-ONE

Under the Same Roof

NOLAN AND STEVE Bushnell weren't brothers (except via their bond at the Pi Kapp house) and probably didn't know each other very well during their time at Pi-K-A. Nolan founded Atari and Chuck E. Cheese after leaving the university, spending some time on the card table in the back room at the frat house along the way. He left about the time Steve arrived. They were both brilliant. Steve and I would bump into each other at the local YMCA, where we liked to play pick-up basketball. Steve could shoot from anywhere on the court, dropping long bombs way before Steph Curry was in grade school. He was a lanky, good-looking blue-eyed kid with blond hair. He looked more like a surfer than a baller. I didn't even know his name when we played ball together or where he was from. I was surprised to see him rush our fraternity, and also surprised when he joined. Later, he dropped out of law school and stopped being my full-time roommate to start a pool cover business in California. Nolan invented Pong, the first-ever commercial video game, while working in the penny arcade area of Lagoon, a local amusement park a half-hour up the road from the frat house. Steve worked part-time for a local guy who had invented a better type of pool cover, which Steve helped install in pools around Salt Lake City. One day Steve said to me, "There are a million swimming pools in California, and none of them have covers that work as well as these." He'd been doing some research between dating girls, shooting hoops and studying law. He liked girls and basketball, but not law school so much. So he left law school, negotiated the rights to sell the pool covers in L.A. and beyond, and moved there with another Pi Kapp, Lanny Smith, who also waved goodbye to law school.

A little less than a decade later, Steve and Lanny were rich. So was Nolan. Nolan retired in California, and Steve and Lanny returned to Utah. Steve and I were roommates again, often staying up late at night to play Nolan's creation, Atari, which was by now a huge sensation, inspiring other video game competitors and changing the world forever. The difference between Steve and me was that now we had both graduated, I had to get up and go to work in the morning at my job downtown. Steve didn't. Steve bought a Cadillac because he liked the car. Steve wore t-shirts and jeans or shorts every day. He was probably the least pretentious guy I knew, especially knowing he likely had millions in a bank somewhere. He didn't seem like a Cadillac-type guy to me. Steve sold the Cadillac not because he didn't like it, but because girls didn't. Before he bought it, I tried to warn him: "How many girls do you think you'll pick up driving a Cadillac?" He bought a BMW which improved his social life a thousand-fold.

We were both labeled "bachelors" not because we wanted to be, but because we couldn't figure out how to get married. In the meantime, we lived a pretty good life together, cooking frozen hamburgers on our patio grill, shooting hoops, playing games on our Atari and, since we didn't find them at the Pi Kapp house, looking for girls to marry. Most of the time we dated different girls, but once in a while, when a girl got tired of one of us, the other would try to pick up the slack. One day Steve said to me, "Mike, I know I'm hopeless, but you're a lost cause. You'll never get married."

Steve and I were among the last bachelors from our era of Pi Kapp life. Lew Bautista, who I hung out with all the way from 8th grade to frat life and beyond, didn't join us in bachelorhood. Lew was the ultimate face man, and he married a cheerleader from our university. Lew started a restaurant that sold soup and breadsticks in town. He was very successful doing it, but he was working his butt off. His day started at about 4 am when he started cooking soup and ended about 8 pm, after he closed the restaurant and counted his money.

One day his brother-in-law said to him, "Lew, it's cold as hell in Minneapolis, and there isn't one place here that makes soup like you do." I hated to see Lew move. I helped him toss his sofa off their second-story balcony, watching it break into pieces on the lawn below, much to the chagrin of his wife the cheerleader. Lew and I were the best of friends. We could almost tell what the other one was thinking, which is why we knew what to do that day on the balcony. We started listening to jazz classics like Miles Davis' *Kind of Blue* in the early '60s on a small stereo in his backyard, and took up playground basketball and tennis during the long, hot summers.

Lew moved a lot. His dad was in real estate, but we kept in touch and remain close friends today. He sold his eight soup restaurants in Minnesota and retired a few years ago to be near his kids. He probably never imagined he would accomplish so much, back when we were bumming around playgrounds and hanging out in our neighborhood late into the night while no one worried about us. He still has that wonderfully intelligent wife, the cheerleader, and a ton of grandkids who love to visit them at their ranch in the mountains of Arizona.

Erv and Walt and Andy migrated to Alaska right after graduating with honors from the Pike house and some degree of learning from the university. I admired them for going there. It was cold and dark and snowed almost all the time. People bought big furry coats and heavy boots. I don't think hardly any girls were there, either. It was nighttime some days for 18 or 20 hours, which would have been perfect for snuggling with girls if any had actually been around. My reasoning was that it was almost like a different planet up there, and unless you liked to hunt and fish, there wouldn't be much to do. Most girls probably thought a lot like me on this.

Erv didn't really have a nickname, but it would have been something along the lines of "Indiana Jones" today. We called Walt "Mitty" after Walter Mitty, the main character in James Thurber's classic short story. In the book and then a couple of movies that followed, Mitty was a dreamer and teller of tall tales. Walt could always dazzle our pledges with stories that rivaled the fictional Walter Mitty. Andy was "C-Note" for reasons I already explained. You wouldn't think of them necessarily as brilliant entrepreneurs or a perfect fit to start a company. I only knew them as screw-offs, like I was back in the fraternity. But they were all of that: brilliant, entrepreneurial, and expert businessmen. Not all at once, but over time, their business ventures unfolded in Alaska. Each brought different talents to their jobs, first starting as salespeople for Xerox. Then as real estate developers for a population that was growing exponentially, with even more girls moving there. And, then as entrepreneurs who ended up in the air freight business in and around Alaska. Erv even found a second niche trading airplane parts for a profit out of Cambodia. (You'll see why Erv was a real-life Indiana Jones later.)

JR, who we affectionately called "110%" Knight, had a way of encouraging his peers to perform at peak levels, something

I needed to hear from time to time. I'm grateful he was there to remind me. JR was a handsome guy and a football player who met his wife after a big game at another school. She was a cheerleader for the other team. More or less, he crossed party lines that day and found a way to end up on the other side of the field so he could meet her. That worked out well, except he married her and left the fold, too. We had been roommates when Bushnell and I were not. I stopped throwing him footballs from about ten feet away at his head or other body parts when he got married. I missed that.

In college JR's entrepreneurial skills began to emerge with the calendar business he and fellow frat brothers, John Lear and Don Bleak started. Lear eventually went off to work for Robert Redford before starting his own company, and Don went into real estate. After college, JR made plenty of money investing in various things and started a financial planning and investment company, and he loved thinking of ways to create "cash flow" for his investors. Cash flow, it turns out, is the essence of survival. Because when you retire, anything you kept up to that point starts going out the back door. Sure, maybe a little at a time. But, like watching the ruptured gas tank empty out of my dad's Oldsmobile with the fins, it starts going away. Into the ground, so to speak. So, in a way, he helped me channel my comparatively small nest egg into some fruitful investments. Not to mention giving 110%.

During my college career, I gained enough knowledge in classes to graduate and start a career, but the brothers of Pi Kappa Alpha gave me perspective, something I wouldn't otherwise have had. Not in the doses available there. Although I've forgotten many of the things I learned in books and by watching professors in classes like History 101 and Algebra 101, I will never forget lessons I learned sitting on the front porch or in the back rooms at 51 North Wolcott. I almost feel sorry for everyone who didn't join a fraternity or sorority and just went to class. I wish they had been required by the university, just like History 101. I can't say fraternity life is for everyone, since I can't stand in everyone else's shoes. But it was a golden time, and I just wish everyone else could be lucky enough to have a hundred friends they could call brothers, all under the same roof, or occasionally on top of it.

TWENTY-TWO

Dead Weight

I WOULDN'T SAY JOINING the Army was a mistake, even though my draft number made it unlikely that I would ever be called to the front lines. I learned something about discipline, doing the little required details that seemed unimportant at the time, but could save someone's life if you were ever in a tight situation. The Army called it being "buttoned up." The full time Army doesn't have room for slackers. "Dead weight" was the other term you heard a lot. The Army doesn't want anyone to be a burden to others in a wartime situation. The same is true for sports, only without the threat of death.

When you are on active duty, things are different than when you're hanging around the command post for weekend training. It was serious when we were on active duty because many of the guys from my barracks were "RA," or Regular Army, and they were getting ready to go to Vietnam to fight an important war for the government, and maybe die. I believe in our government, but they were dead wrong on this, and it cost too much in lives lost (over 60,000). I'm finding as I get older that our government is often wrong on war. There are times not to fight, and there are times when it appears there is no choice. I think we should have a strong military so people in other countries think twice about picking a fight with us. The other thing is that it's important to fight a war we can win, usually on our terms. That wasn't the case in Vietnam.

Back in our home barracks at Fort Douglas, we weren't as nervous about going to war. We probably should have been. For the moment, things were much more relaxed, and so we sought a little diversion now and then.

Sleeping during these weekend training sessions wasn't an option unless you were able to find some place you never thought anyone would look. That was usually off the base and came with some degree of risk, unless you could find an empty cardboard box wide and long enough to accommodate a soldier. And we did. It was in John Nelson's supply room. Nellie had been assigned to the supply room because they would know where to find him very easily. But when he showed us the box, Pat Roylance kept eyeing it, remembering the time the First Sergeant found him at his home. Maybe this would turn out better. Even though we couldn't check a pillow and blanket out of the supply room, which was relegated to things like shovels and latrine pills, Pat climbed in, thinking it would be better than walking around trying to look busy. I don't remember how long Pat was in the box but long enough to take off his contact lenses and curl up a little. And I would never have guessed that an officer would walk through the supply room, tell us to "carry on"—which meant to get back to work doing who knows what—and then for some inexplicable reason, casually lift the lid on the box as he walked by and peek into it.

I've seen double-takes before, but maybe not as good as this one. If an iPhone had been invented back then, a recording would have gone viral. Pretty soon, but not real soon, Pat was standing at attention so the officer could "dress him down," which is short for verbally undressing him in front of everyone else. I think Pat, standing very stiff and straight up, tried to salute without much success. He had been in the box for a while, and he looked a little groggy. Later, Pat told me he couldn't really see who was talking to him because he had removed his contact lenses, but he knew he was important because of the silver emblems that seemed to be watching him from the shoulders of whoever it was standing right in front of him.

Another time when boredom got the best of us, visiting "Nellie" in his supply room, we got another brilliant idea. Nellie had been a little flippant with us that day, probably teasing us about not having a supply room to hang out in like he did. So, we took some masking tape and began wrapping his legs together, and then tied his arms behind his back. The second idea we had was to tape his mouth shut and then put a helmet over him. The helmet comes in two parts, as you know if you've ever had any military experience. The first part is the liner. It fits over your head nicely and then the steel pot goes over it. That's to keep the bullets from penetrating your head, which could come in handy. They're supposed to ricochet off the metal pot. However, if you wear the pot without the liner, it almost completely covers your head. It's like having no neck, but just a big metal pot on your shoulders. At the very least, the image it evokes giggles from observers in the area, especially if you tape the steel pot to someone's head. That is, until a very alert superior officer walks in the room, and after noticing the activity right in front of him on the expansive supply room floor, yells, "ATTTENNTTTCHUNN!"

Of course, we all did what we were asked to do: stand up straight and salute the officer. Unfortunately, Nellie could neither stand up nor salute. Or see what was happening. I tried to help him by ripping off some of the tape so he could see. But all I did was scratch his face as I tried to remove his big, green steel pot which was pretty much fastened to his head. I had actually done a pretty good job of taping him up, something I hadn't really learned during training and probably wouldn't ever use again. So John did what I probably would have done; he tried to hop away and disappear. Into thin air. But it was a big room. John knew that, and he kept hopping blindly along anyway. Abruptly the officer, along with a couple of other officer type guys he brought with him, turned and left the room. We never heard from them again. Reportedly, they were laughing so hard they had to stop and lean against a wall while they wiped tears from their eyes. I thought it would be interesting if their commanding officer accidentally came along and called them to ATTTENNNTCHUN.

Our first experience with actual Army life came at Camp Roberts, which was a lot like Fort Irwin, nestled pretty close to Death Valley, but maybe even hotter. Fort Irwin is where we stole the tire off the major's jeep, did maneuvers in jeeps all day long, and snuck into the base to watch *The Dirty Dozen*. Before that we went to Camp Roberts. That was the place Nellie's dad the recruiter said we would "get" to go to if we hurried and joined the Army. I thought about Nellie's dad a lot while we were there, in Death Valley.

Here's how it was at Camp Roberts: the average temperature was 105 degrees in the day, and 104 degrees at night. For this reason, the Army decided to have us train in two four-hour stints: from midnight to 4 am when it was a little cooler, and then again from 8 am to noon, when it was getting warmer. Then we got the rest of the day off. So, from noon to midnight, we were on our own. The problem was that the barracks we were supposed to stay in and have time to ourselves were made of shiny metal, and I think the average temperature inside them was about 120 degrees. I remember laying on a bunk bed as still as I possibly could, while pools of sweat accumulated on my stomach and forehead and drained into the mattress underneath me. I'm just glad the others in the barracks didn't know that it was my friends and I who started the rumor we were going to have to spend an additional two weeks at Camp Roberts because of an airline strike.

Of course, this is nothing compared to what soldiers go through today. All of the above, and the possibility of driving over a land mine in Iraq, being downed by a helicopter in Somalia, being picked off by a sniper in Afghanistan, or any number of acts of violence against our country and its brave men and women. *"How did we get here?"* I often ask myself.

TWENTY-THREE

The Heat

HEAT WAS AN enigma. He looked like a tall, blonde Swedish model, with a model-type body to go with a model-type face and a year-round suntan. He was probably six feet tall. He just showed up one day, joined the fraternity and then soon moved into the house. We learned that he had played AAA baseball in California and could throw fast ball pitches at around 100 mph with some degree of accuracy. So we called him "Heat." I didn't know much more about him other than how he earned his nickname. Maybe some of the guys knew something, but Jon Lervig didn't divulge much. He had girlfriends, of course, and he was very amiable and easy-going. We liked him. Liked having him around. He seemed to mysteriously come and go. One minute he was there, and the next minute he wasn't. The only thing that alerted us to Jon being around was the motorcycle with no muffler that he showed up with one day and kept for a while. Otherwise, he was quiet when it came to talking about anything too personal.

I have two memories of him while we both lived in the house. Earlier, I recounted the story of him throwing three snowballs through my upstairs bedroom window, that was cracked maybe two inches open to let some cold air in while I attempted to study at my desk right under it. Those snowballs came so quickly, one after the other, that I couldn't imagine how one guy was able to throw them even if they were pre-formed and ready to go. And here's the amazing thing: somehow Heat was able to squeeze every one of them through that two-inch opening, leaving a little splatter on the glass while the rest, now slightly busted open on impact, whizzed into my room. I had never really doubted him, but that night he gave me real proof that he had been aptly nicknamed "Heat." You wanted him on your team if it came to throwing baseballs or snowballs or just about anything else.

The other experience was a little more delicate. John smoked a joint now and then. So did some of the other brothers. It was a product you could quite easily acquire. Or grow. I didn't have a problem with people smoking marijuana. Stoned guys were quite easy to be around. The problem was that in between studying, throwing snowballs, relaxing around the house, hanging out with girls and smoking marijuana, Heat was also growing it. In the backyard of the frat house. And, that was illegal at the time. As president of the fraternity that year (the official title was "SMC" and I had no idea what that meant), I told him he just couldn't do that. For obvious reasons, like jail time, or losing our charter. And some pretty unfavorable publicity that could accompany being exposed. We chatted one night, and he readily agreed to dig up those little plants and get rid of them. And he did that. I kept an eye on the backyard fence line after that, and the Heat was probably doing other things, but one of them was not growing marijuana in the backyard.

One night several months later while we were shooting the breeze in his room, I noticed a cake pan from the kitchen underneath his bed. Little green sprouts were protruding from it, surrounded by carefully cultivated dirt. They didn't look edible. "Jon," I pleaded, "In the house? That's even worse! You know you can't do this. If somehow you got caught, we'd all be in big trouble. At least if you're growing it outside, you might claim that someone else had borrowed our yard for that purpose." And that was that. At least as far as I know. Occasionally I wondered if anyone else might have been borrowing cake pans from the kitchen, using them for some reason other than baking.

What brought Heat to the Pi Kapp House was throwing his arm out playing professional baseball. Hondo said he used to play catch with Heat in the backyard on warm spring afternoons. Maybe it brought back memories for Heat. Other guys played catch, too, but not for long. "He was simply unbelievable," said Hondo. "You lived in fear that if you missed his throw, awful things could happen to you. He could throw that hard." Heat still had it. He could still "bring the heat" at just a little less than 100 mph. Maybe his arm got sore after a while and he couldn't last enough innings in the big leagues to stick. One thing we all knew: Heat could throw. And throw hard. You didn't want to be on the receiving end without a well-padded mitt.

"Alone in the world," is how one brother described him. I wish I had known Jon better. Maybe he didn't have a history that had been kind to him, or maybe he just didn't feel the need to share much. But he was a brother; well liked. And, not just for his baking expertise. I don't know how far he went in school. That's not important. He's doing something he loves today: managing his fishing guide business and being a family man somewhere in Alaska. Plenty of snowballs to toss around up there. And maybe a few cracked open windows to zing them through.

1967

The invention of the Big Mac

In 1967, the actor Ronald Reagan was elected as governor of California. 10,000 people protested the Vietnam War in San Francisco. Dr. James Bedford became the first person put in a special deep freeze state with the intent of someday being scientifically resuscitated. His revival date hasn't been announced. The Green Bay Packers defeated the Kansas City Chiefs 35-10 in the first ever Super Bowl. Gus Grissom, Ed White and Roger Chafee died when a fire started inside their spacecraft during a launchpad test at Cape Canaveral. The Doors released their self-titled first album. The American Basketball Association was formed, and the LA Stars moved to Utah under new owner Bill Daniels. Joseph Stalin's daughter defected to the United States. The first Boeing 737 took off. The 25th Amendment was added to the US Constitution, which says what will happen if a US President or Vice President dies or is removed from office. Robert McNamara resigned as Secretary of Defense after President Johnson refused to end the Vietnam War by turning fighting over to the South Vietnamese. McDonald's introduced the Big Mac. Israel defeated Palestine in the Six Day War. Bell bottoms were bigger than ever, and the mini-skirt got a little shorter. So did short-shorts. Men were going in the opposite direction when it came to haircuts, and some of us even stopped getting them. *The Graduate, Bonnie and Clyde* and *Cool Hand Luke* were considered groundbreaking movies, aimed at younger audiences. And the Vietnam War got bigger. And worse. Not a great year when you consider The Big Mac might have been our shining moment.

TWENTY-FOUR
The Sneak, Part II

YOU COULDN'T MISS the large blackboard just inside the front door of 51 North Wolcott. Credit my brothers for never writing anything obscene or in poor taste on it as far as I can remember. It was reserved for important messages, and mostly for upcoming PI Kapp soirees. And "Peach Days," which Rex (soon to be "U-Haul") Johnson had concocted, was gathering momentum. Who was Peaches? How did Rex ever find her? Were there any pictures of her dancing around in her exotic dance costume? Would she dance in the Pi Kapp living room? Who was coming to the party to celebrate Peach Days with Peaches? That kind of discussion started filling up the lunch room almost every day. Rex started answering questions on the large blackboard, and the brothers started watching as Peaches began to take shape. He may have even introduced a couple of unbelieving brothers to Peaches near one of the locations she frequented as a performer, which added to the credibility and subsequently the momentum of the upcoming occasion.

The date was sometime in May, I think. Brothers had to pay $25 to cover the costs of food, beverages, and Peaches, the now famous exotic dancer. There was an urgency that came with the message: Peaches was on retainer, but if she got a better offer, we'd lose out. Money started flowing. Rex smiled and told everyone not to worry. Peaches was on the way.

However, within a few days or maybe a week, as chapter president, I told Rex I was worried about having the party at the house. I didn't want to be the one who said Peaches couldn't dance for my Pi Kapp brothers, but Rex quickly agreed with me. I was surprised he did. A few days later at lunch, Rex made the announcement to the brothers that the party was off. I don't think he even mentioned my name, but he said there was concern about complications if Peaches was found out. The brothers were not happy. They told Rex they weren't happy, too, in so many words. Rex seemed to cower a little, knowing he'd set up a party that might not happen. He seemed penitent. He told the brothers to hold on. He'd try to figure something out. Just looking in his eyes, you could tell his mind was visibly on the move.

The thing that justified canceling the party was the other party we'd had with another exotic dancer in the living room of the Pi Kapp house. I don't think she was friends with Peaches, but she could really dance around quite well while removing some of her clothing. I think her name was Jeri. Scott and Don, our social chairmen at the time, had found her dancing around in Park City and put the party together. Many, but not all of the brothers, lined up along the walls of the living room to give her enough room to dance. A keg was just outside the front door, and it was emptied pretty quickly, which led to the demise of the party. After a few remarks early on from the gallery that weren't very complimentary, Jeri grabbed her discarded clothing (which wasn't a lot) and ran out the front door in tears. The big problem here was that she didn't want to drive her pink Cadillac home. She wanted a driver.

As house president, I was quickly elected. The brothers might have even promised me another term if I did it. Not that I was interested in that. But, since our house was in the middle of a neighborhood full of people and families, it didn't look good having an exotic dancer running out the front door crying. So I did it. Reluctantly.

First off, just like the pink Cadillac, Jeri wasn't my type. She was a pretty girl, but not the girl I was looking for. Secondly, I wasn't thinking things through as well as I should have. I quickly got her in the pink Cadillac and drove off, making sure the neighbors weren't around as I headed the car towards downtown somewhere. It was then I realized that I hadn't asked any of the brothers to follow me so I could have a ride back. But Jeri turned out to be a sweet girl, with lots of feelings which bubbled through the mascara running down her face. She was just trying to make ends meet, she said. I wondered a little how the pink Cadillac worked into things, but I took her at her word. Miraculously, everything turned out pretty good, all things considered. Her boyfriend gave me a ride back to the frat house. Scott and Don had pre-paid her for hosting the party; we removed the keg from the front porch so the neighbors wouldn't take photos and send them to the dean's office, and everyone went back to studying or doing other harmless things that night. Jeri was back with her boyfriend. Everyone seemed happy again. Except maybe a couple of brothers who blamed a couple of other brothers for getting drunk and loose-tongued around Jeri. They didn't want her to feel bad, I guess.

TWENTY-FIVE

Dream Girls

A "DREAM GIRL" WAS a young woman we brothers held in very high esteem. We elected a new one every year, putting them on a pedestal the best we could. Most other fraternities did what we did: they chose someone they thought was pretty, and also pretty smart, to represent them and show others we were pretty good guys after all. None of our Dream Girls ever danced around in the Pi Kapp living room. None of them drove pink Cadillacs, although I dated a terrific girl whose parents had a pink Cadillac she drove once in a while, and she would have been a perfect Dream Girl. She just wasn't fond enough of me or my Pi Kapp brothers to run for Dream Girl at the time.

It was a pretty sure bet that most Dream Girls would end up marrying a Pi Kapp and live happily ever after. Kathy Hulbert was one of my favorite Dream Girls but she ended up marrying Roger Penske, the billion-dollar racecar driver, and lived happily ever after with him. We were all okay with that for the most part, because it made the rest of us look pretty good having known her as our Dream Girl. Rebecca Marriott was one of the other girls who didn't marry a Pi Kapp. But she

LOVED us. She and I became good friends when she was our Dream Girl because I was the house president, and we talked a lot about the things she wanted to do for the brothers. The great thing was she knew most of us pretty well, and she knew that we weren't perfect. Far from perfect. She probably even knew about Jeri dancing around in our living room, but she forgave us and loved us anyway. "Rebby" was a high-class Chi Omega sorority girl, with great taste in just about everything from clothes to cars and anything in between. Like all our Dream Girls, she was a dream to look at. I was always a little surprised she loved us so much. Most of us were probably thinking she could do better.

Rebby showed up all the time and didn't care what we looked like at any particular moment. That's a pretty good indication of true love, in my book. She brought cookies and cakes for birthdays, and attended our chapter meetings from time to time. And she came to all our parties, except The Bowery, which you'll learn about a little later. She was "there for us" as they say, and we loved how much attention and cheering up she gave us. She was always lining us up with Chi Omegas or other girls around campus. The night we voted for Dream Girl that year, U-Haul Johnson and I were counting the votes in my room. It came down to Rebby and one other girl who was also terrific. It was a win-win situation with either of them. But Rex and I worried that maybe Rebecca would be out of our league and not as interested in being our Dream Girl after a few months. Only one vote separated the two of them. But Rebecca won. We pondered the outcome for a few minutes. We recounted the votes just to make sure. And then Rebecca Marriott became the best Dream Girl you could ever ask for.

Every year we had The Dream Girl Formal, which was very first-class. And big. It lasted almost all day, usually with some water skiing and breakfast or lunch, and then a black-tie dinner affair complete with a nice gift for each girlfriend who came with us. I remember taking my favorite girl, the one who didn't own a pink Cadillac but just drove her parents' around once in a while. We doubled with Lee Smith, one of my Pi Kapp pledge brothers who was always good for some laughs. It was a wonderful day from start to finish, except that Lee brought some kind of homebrewed drink that he spilled in the trunk of my dad's Oldsmobile with the fins on the back. Luckily it evaporated and didn't leave much of a stain. Of course, we always honored our Dream Girl, bringing her up on the stage of the dance floor, giving her roses and maybe even a crown, and then serenading her with our favorite song about being a Pi Kapp. Not the song that had the line, "I love my Johnny Walker and I love my lady's leg"—the other one about being a good fraternity man and honoring the women we loved.

The only other Dream Girl I knew personally was "pinned" to Bob Woolf, who I admired a lot. His girlfriend was ever so classy. Well-spoken. Demure. And maybe a little quiet even though she was a cheerleader at the university. She was the prototype for what a Dream Girl should be. Getting pinned had nothing to do with the term used in wrestling, although that kind of activity might help encourage two people to decide that getting pinned was probably the next step in their relationship. When that happened, we had a ceremony at the girl's home, or her sorority if she was in one. We'd all stand around by the fireplace or a piano with candles and serenade the girl, "serenade" being a loose term for a bunch of guys, and then our brother would pin a Pi Kapp emblem to her dress and give her a kiss. Getting pinned was pretty serious, because it usually meant the next step was getting engaged, graduating, and then getting married and going off to medical school or some other cool place. Which is pretty much what Bob and our Dream Girl, Gail did. I liked that idea but knew there was no way I was getting into med school or law school or pretty much any other school after I graduated. And I wasn't sure what my own Dream Girl would really look like or be. Not at this point. I knew I had a lot of work to do, even though I really liked the girl who occasionally drove her parents' pink Cadillac. PS: Frat brother Norm Anderson, nonchalant and somewhat elusive, dated two of our dream girls but didn't marry either one. They seemed okay with that.

TWENTY-SIX

Basic Stuff

EVEN THOUGH WE were part-time soldiers, we had to spend some full-time in the Regular Army getting trained, just in case Vietnam called us to come over there. We never thought it would become a reality, although it almost did. But lots of other things happened to me in the meantime, while I was on "active" duty.

It all started in October 1966 when I was shipped off to Fort Lewis in Seattle, Washington for what the army calls "Basic Training," also referred to as "Basic Combat Training" or BCT. I was 19. My parents drove me to the airport and said goodbye. I think I was more sad leaving than they were seeing me go. It was cold and wet in Washington when I got there. I'd gone from 110 degrees in the desert heat of Camp Roberts and Fort Irwin to less than 50-degree temperatures, perennially overcast skies, and mud puddles from the constant rain that fell all over Fort Lewis. I would soon be crawling around in the mud puddles, shooting guns and throwing grenades. The grenades weren't real, but the guns were. Right away they gave us all a bunch of things we'd need to wear on top of our uniforms, like rain gear and ponchos with their own hoods that fit snuggly over our steel pot helmets. And, shots. Lots of shots in the arms, given mostly by guys who really didn't look like they had any idea what they were doing. And, it felt that way, too.

I was assigned to a company of soldiers, and we had our own barracks. We had 24 or more guys sleeping in bunk beds. I think I was on the top bunk, and a guy named Snowden, also from Utah, was on the bottom bunk. He was really a great guy, which made it easier being a soldier. I can't remember his first name, but he was a private like me, and that's all our drill sergeant ever called any of us. "Private." He rarely got any of our last names right when he tried. I have never heard so many different pronunciations of my own name. And the interesting thing about that is there is only one vowel in my entire last name. I can't remember his last name either.

One of the first things I noticed was that the bathroom was just one big room, with some shower heads sticking out of the walls and a bunch of toilets sticking out of the floor. Even the toilets at the frat house offered some privacy. But maybe that's how the Army went about developing togetherness among its soldiers. Enough about that, though.

Like I said, our drill sergeant was pretty strict. He would inspect us all the time and sometimes tear someone's bed apart because the top blanket wasn't squared off and tucked in correctly. He was a lot stricter than my wife would be years later on this rule. Plus, we spent what seemed like hours polishing our shoes, or polishing the brass buttons on our uniforms, sometimes late into the night. I knew they were just going to get all muddy the next day, but that didn't seem to bother our sergeant. He also liked to inspect our lockers to make sure we hadn't smuggled anything in we weren't supposed to have. One time he discovered a box of chocolates from the girlfriend of one of our bunkmates. He made the guy eat the whole box of chocolates, two layers' worth, while we stood around and watched. He spent some time after that in the big bathroom I was telling you about. Stuff like this went on for the eight weeks we were stationed there, getting our "basic training" in before we were shipped to the next base for "advanced infantry training" or AIT.

One day while out with my platoon, our drill sergeant pointed to another platoon just across the way. They looked a little different than us. They just seemed to stumble along, looking very tired. Our drill sergeant told us these were the guys that didn't make it through basic training, and had to do it again. They had been "recycled." He didn't have to say any more to us for the rest of the day, or find a reason to get mad at us. Nothing like a nice visual lesson to help you understand the urgency of your current situation, I thought. The other thought I had was that if you had to take basic training twice, how much better would you be the second time? Wouldn't you be even more tired, and perhaps be thinking about the possibility of taking it a third time? I wondered if anyone had ever spent their entire military career in basic training. Then I stopped thinking about the do-over company and decided it would just be best not to qualify in any way for a do-over. I had always thought a do-over was something you *wanted* to do, so you could get it better the next time. That is, until then.

Of course, nighttime brought a whole new set of challenges related to sleeping. Imagine a room full of a couple dozen guys trying to sleep in bunk beds from 9 pm to 5 am. Then, off in the distance someone would start blowing a trumpet. That meant our drill sergeant would soon be standing at the end of the room, smiling, like he relished the idea of torturing us for the next 15 hours or so. Most of us were dead tired because there were always one or two guys who had been talking in their sleep, or snoring loudly most of the night. You might also hear guys getting up and heading to the bathroom in the middle of the night, looking for a little time alone.

Daytime was filled with drills and maneuvers, although "maneuvers" is a misnomer because you're really not moving in any kind of strategic fashion. It seemed like we were either marching or standing around, waiting for someone to give us something else to do. One of my least favorite queues was the line we waited in to try out gas masks. You put your gas mask on after adjusting it to fit tightly around your face, making sure the vents on the front of it were closed properly. Then on command, you entered the gas chamber and walked through it to the other side. Of course, the odds weren't great you'd get everything just right before you walked through the chamber and out the other side, seeing soldiers gasping and coughing for dear life, just like you. The world was right to ban gas attacks in warfare.

The other line I remember most was the chow line. I had a love-hate relationship with that line, because what often happened was when you were so extremely hungry you could hardly make it to the serving table, you inevitably found out that liver was the main course. And probably cauliflower or some other less desirable vegetable as a sidekick to the liver. Conversely, when you'd been sitting around all morning getting lectures after a big breakfast, the Army served your favorite lunch which you could hardly choke down. It was just the way they did things. It was extremely well-planned.

After eight weeks of not getting any sleep, crawling around in the mud with guns (mostly under rain that never quit), and sitting in foxholes or on benches, I became sick. I couldn't wait to get home and sleep in a real bed without any squared-off corners. I could see the end of basic training coming! To wrap things up, though, our drill sergeant announced what he called a "twelve-mile forced march." With full equipment, backpacks, commando boots, rifles, steel helmets, and maybe a couple of other things. We had already run a mile once for time. I think you had to make it in under ten minutes or you faced marching with the platoon of second-timers. By now we had all developed a little comradery, probably as much from sharing the bathroom as crawling around in the mud, so we all celebrated a bit when that mile was over. I wondered how we would all fare doing twelve miles. Especially with our drill sergeant watching us, thinking maybe some of us would fit nicely in the other, do-over company. I wondered if he might even have some kind of a quota on this.

As far as I can remember, I think all of us got through and graduated from basic training. But boy were we all sore from jogging twelve miles in army boots and wearing a bunch of other military stuff. One of our guys was a farm boy from Idaho. He loved the Army way of life other than that he completely missed his wife, who he said took really good care of him in every way. He was one of the fittest guys in our company, and he proved it by actually running around most of us as he headed to the front of the line, wearing a big, cheesy grin all the time. Sometimes he dropped back just so he could feel the pleasure of running around us a second time. You knew he was coming because his canteen must have been loose, and it jingled a lot on his belt as he flashed that big, toothy grin at you. I'm sure the Army felt bad when his tour of duty was up. Maybe his wife did, too. They probably felt really good about my leaving the military way of life, however.

When I got home, I spent two weeks in bed during Christmastime. My mom gave me lots of soup and tucked in my bedsheets for me, usually with me in them. It was a wonderful reprieve, and it just shows you how much parents are willing to do to help you. But I knew I had to get ready for eight more weeks of training. This time in tanks and jeeps at

Fort Knox, Kentucky. America was headed into 1967, it was still wintertime, and I had visions of me crawling around in snow and ice instead of mud puddles. It's probably good that I didn't know my draft number would be 195 when they would draw it a couple years from then in the first military draft, and that maybe I could have avoided all this Army stuff.

TWENTY-SEVEN

Social Life

DRINKING IS A favorite frat house pastime. At my house, about half the brothers drank, and about half didn't. That's probably a bit unusual, but it meant a guy could be comfortable hanging around the house drunk or sober.

There weren't any house rules about when guys could drink or not. It was a judgment call. Sometimes a brother or two had to intercede or help out a little if someone overdid it, helping him to his room or the patio or maybe an upstairs bathroom.

This is where brotherhood became a big thing. Brotherhood meant you were okay with all of your brothers, even though they might occasionally make fools of themselves, drunk or sober. As things went, I wasn't above making a fool of myself, either. The reality is that anytime you run into fifty guys hanging out together, drunk or sober or even partially drunk *and* sober, just about anything can happen.

But, don't get the wrong idea. Frat life at the Pi Kapp house wasn't anything like you hear about or watch in movies like *Animal House*. Well, actually, *Animal House* with the late John Belushi wasn't too far off. It just wasn't a big two-hour movie full of drinking and pranking. Things like that could happen, perhaps, but over time. Yes, we had some guys who could crush beer cans on their foreheads, for instance. And we had our version of their famous toga party, called The Bowery, and there were other goings-on that occasionally got the attention of the deans sitting in offices over on campus. Sometimes the neighbors took pictures of the fraternity house the next morning after one of our parties and sent them to the dean. The photos could be pretty convincing that any particular party had been a success, depending how you looked at it.

One time, a couple of our guys ended up sleeping on the roof. If I remember correctly, there may have been an empty keg on the front porch, too. Not too long after those pictures arrived on his desk, I ended up in the dean's office, trying to explain things away. The dean listened but told me to tell the others that it better not happen again, unless we wanted to face some rather dire consequences. I think the guys sleeping on the roof were concerning to him as it didn't represent exemplary frat house behavior. I was hoping for a little more understanding, but he didn't act like he had ever been to a fraternity party. I couldn't blame the neighbors, though. They put up with a lot over the years because it seemed like something was always happening, planned or not, at the busiest house on the street. Luckily, neither the dean nor the neighbors heard about active brother Paul Gamble building his own ski jump on the roof of the frat house in the middle of winter, or watched him land head first in a snow bank just beyond the patio. I didn't see it happen, either, but evidently Paul got a little too far over his ski tips once he was airborne. Otherwise, witnesses said his form was perfect. Hope he was wearing goggles.

On the whole, our parties were pretty tame, especially if we brought dates. That's when we tried to be on our best behavior, although it wasn't easy to define what that meant, exactly. One of the more memorable parties was the annual Cajun Party, held in the living room of the house, and it came complete with swamp decorations, including a small makeshift stream that ran through the living room. We served Cajun food and danced to Jamaican-type music. Big tree-like plants were positioned throughout, leaving a little room for the Jamaican-type group that played and sang through the trees by the front room window. I was glad when I wasn't a pledge anymore and didn't have to clean up after these parties the next day.

When Dick Lybert, from my pledge class, was social chairman for the fraternity, he tried to upstage that Cajun Party with a Beach Party. Dick drove a brand-new Camaro and usually parked it right in front of the house, trying to showcase us being fancy car guys, but he moved his beloved NASCAR-looking machine with nearly 500 horsepower so a large dump truck could bring in about a half ton of sand which was dispersed into the living room. Most of us felt like Dick missed it a little on this party, because the sand became a problem for over a month after the party was over. First of all, the sand didn't stay in the living room where it was supposed to be. It was tracked throughout the rest of the house and up the stairs into bedrooms and bathrooms, where it managed to find its way into closets and even toilets and sinks and shower drains. Secondly, the frat house living room had a big rug that covered some of the hardwood floor but not all of it. Hardwood floors don't take naturally to sand. We spent months accidentally grinding the remaining sand into the cracks in the floor as we walked through the living room area. I concluded that the only time it was really great having sand all around you was when you actually were on a beach. I wished Dick would have applied the cost of the sand to a real beach party somewhere a little more exotic than our front room.

Dick continued to park his souped-up Camaro right next to the front door of the frat house, until one night when Rod Shelton and Doc Bates—both a little blitzed from a downtown stint at the Joker Lounge—decided they wanted that same parking spot, but forgetting perhaps that Dick's Camaro was already there. It would have been an ideal photo-op for our unhappy neighbors.

I don't remember much about all the other parties we had, but I know we had a Casino Night, complete with several different gaming tables we positioned around the house. "C-Note" Anderson, Nolan Bushnell and others made this a fun party to watch unless you felt like taking them on. If you weren't careful, it could cost you next semester's tuition and maybe even more. We also held our classy Dream Girl Formal night where many of us wore tuxedos, trying to impress the girls we might think about marrying, with a nice big banquet full of food much better than we ate at the frat house. We also had a Fifties Party and talked John Nordquist into being a disc jockey for the evening, and a number of other parties and sorority exchanges that filled our social calendar from October to June.

For the record, Nordquist, one of the funniest guys I've ever known, didn't make it to the end of the Fifties Party. I remember about three or four guys lifting him and carrying him overhead with his arms dangling by his sides, unconscious, on the way up the stairs to his bedroom. This all happened soon after he started singing his own version of "Johnny B. Goode" and passed out onto the turntable. Maybe he was improvising a little too much. I can't remember for sure, but I believe the party kept going for a while. John stole the show early on; and as long as the music was still playing, most people soon forgot he was gone.

Like I said, social life was pretty fun at the frat house.

Something was always going on or just about to. Twenty guys living under the same roof, unless they slept on top of it, without any parental supervision, created a dynamic, ever-changing environment we all clung to as long as possible. Besides, the neighbors were usually watching over us, looking out for our best interests, more or less.

1968

World interrupted

Of all of the years in the Sixties, I think 1968 was the worst. So many sad things happened. Dr. Martin Luther King Jr. was shot and killed. Robert Kennedy was shot and killed. Two of the nation's and probably the world's very best leaders, taken away before they had finished their work. Just like that. First, King was shot by a sniper as he left a motel in April. Thousands mourned and protested in the streets all over the United States for days following King's death. Kennedy was killed in the back of a hotel kitchen surrounded by security people on a hot summer night. He had recently told America he was going to run for President. In between, America committed a total of 549,000 soldiers to fight in Vietnam, using North Vietnam's rules more or less. The North Vietnamese launched the Tet Offensive too, which just created more serious fighting. Soon Viet Cong soldiers attacked the US embassy, killing two guards. Walter Cronkite even suggested it might be time for a truce on *The CBS Evening News* one night. In so many words, he said that maybe our country should try for peace, having done our best to defend democracy. It may have been the first time a media giant set national policy. It wouldn't be the last. "If I lose Cronkite, I've lost Middle America," said President Johnson. Soon he decided not to run for reelection. His idea for a "Great Society" didn't look so good anymore. Especially to all the young people who wondered if they'd even get a chance at the "good life."

As if we didn't have enough trouble, North Korea seized the USS *Pueblo* with 83 American sailors on board saying it was spying on them. One sailor was killed during the attack. North Korea tortured their captives regularly and even put their commander through a mock firing squad. He still didn't confess. Later Captain Bucher and his crew were released after intense negotiations. But the ship still remains in North Korea, somewhere.

A B-52 bomber crashed near Greenland with four nuclear missiles on board. Our country tried to keep it on the downlow, but that didn't last long. Luckily, the nuclear bombs didn't explode. A nuclear submarine, the USS *Scorpion*, sank near the Azores with 99 men on board. A graphic photo of a South Vietnamese soldier executing a North Vietnamese soldier was seen around the world. Some say it was the nail in the coffin for the US in Vietnam. Towards the end of the year, President Johnson stopped bombing North Vietnam.

Three US astronauts got to see the far side of the Moon from their Apollo 7 spacecraft, but Pink Floyd wouldn't release their number one album *Dark Side of the Moon* until a few years later.

John Wesley Carlos and Tommie Smith, US track and field stars at the 1968 Olympics in Mexico City, raised their black-gloved fists to protest the way America was treating its Black citizens, as they stood on the podium after winning the gold and bronze medals in the 100 meter dash. The Black Panthers started toting automatic weapons to protest police brutality in Oakland. Many of us wondered where this was headed. Things got violent several times in confrontations with police. People died. They tried to do some good things, too, like sponsoring lunches for school children and fighting tuberculosis, but that got overshadowed by the violence that seemed to show up wherever they did. So, Governor Ronald Reagan banned the carrying of weapons in public. The Zodiac Killer wasn't listening, though, and was believed to have killed two more people that year in San Francisco.

There was also the Chicago 7, who were charged with

inciting a riot during the Democratic National Convention in the summer of 1968. Abbie Hoffman (who took his own life in 1989), Tom Hayden, Jerry Rubin and others went there to protest the Vietnam War. The trial dragged on for months, through much of the next year, while more and more people began demonstrating in the streets in support of the seven defendants. When it was finally over, even though most of those on trial were initially convicted, all the charges were eventually overturned when it became evident that the police may have even been the ones to start the riots. It was another dark moment.

During 1968, the worldwide flu pandemic killed over 100,000 Americans, coming all the way from Hong Kong on flights to New York and other US destinations. Over a million people died all over the world. Back in America, we watched Stanley Kubrick's movie *2001: A Space Odyssey*. Being on another planet never looked better. Some have compared that year to 2020 with parallels in politics, religion, racial upheaval, world unrest, protests and even a pandemic.

1968 was such a difficult year, the famous composer Luciano Berio hurriedly wrote and performed "Sinfonia," his illustrious work symbolizing one of the worst years in modern history and his hope for the future. One critic called it a "miraculously exhilarating breath of fresh air."

Maybe the Green Bay Packers winning the Super Bowl and the Detroit Tigers winning the World Series helped cheer people up. At least the actor Will Smith was born, and so was skateboard champion Tony Hawk. Larry Sanger was born, too. In case you're wondering who he is, he started Wikipedia. Larry's people wrote about all this stuff that happened in 1968 on his website. He probably could have taught my History 101 class if he had been older.

TWENTY-EIGHT

The Sneak, Part III

THE GREATEST SNEAK in the history of fraternities was still taking shape in Rex's head. I'm not even sure he had an endgame picture of how it would turn out. The idea was to rope in as many brothers-to-be as possible with a too-good-to-be true-sounding party. And have them pay for it. It would have been a great school project for some psychology class at the university.

Within a week or so of telling all the brothers in the lunch room the party was off because we couldn't risk losing our charter as a university sanctioned fraternity house, Rex announced his new plan: moving the party to another location. Seems he had a friend who lived not far away in his parents' home, and that, ironically, they would be out of town in a couple of weeks. We could take the party there, said his friend, as long as he could attend, too. "Brilliant," said everyone, almost in unison. You could feel the energy in the room building as Rex unveiled the plan. More people signed up. Someone drew some peaches on the blackboard in the frat house lobby next to Peaches' name.

It wasn't long, though, before Rex introduced another snag in the biggest fraternity event of the year. His friend wanted a little extra cash to cover any damages as a result of Peaches dancing around in his parents' living room. In hindsight, this was a test. It was a kind of turning point in the whole affair. The brothers could have easily said "no thanks," erased the colorful peach artwork from the blackboard, and walked away. But they didn't. They had turned the corner. Even though the expenses were mounting up, just like they did in the movie *The Hot Rock* with Robert Redford (where the cost of stealing an expensive diamond for an African Chief kept increasing), the brothers were in too deep, and the cost seemed almost reasonable. Like something they would have done if it had been their own parents' living room filled with a bunch of whooping and hollering frat boys. Not to mention Peaches. When you looked at it from this perspective, you might be surprised Rex had been able to convince his friend about the benefits of having the party in the first place. What were a few more dollars per man, anyway? Rex said how grateful his friend would be for their generosity, as he collected everyone's money.

Audaciously, Rex wasn't done toying with the thoughts and feelings of the active brothers in the frat house. No, not at all. He was going to push the limits and test brotherhood even further. And he did that a week or so later. The date of the party, just around the corner, had been written on the blackboard, next to the artistic rendering of some peaches in a bowl. Enthusiasm was just about to peak, when one day, dejected and angry, Rex made another important announcement in the frat house dining room over lunch: *the party was off.* It turned out his friend had gotten cold feet. Ice cold feet. Not even a free keg of beer as a token of appreciation from Rex himself was enough to persuade him otherwise. The thought of a dozen or maybe even two dozen cars pulling up to his parents' home on a Friday afternoon, providing their curious neighbors with countless photo opportunities as a throng of college-aged men walked blatantly over their own private, well-manicured lawns and disappeared into their best friend's home, caused him first to shudder and then panic as he imagined the consequences. The party was NOT GOING TO HAPPEN. End of story.

Sadness and despair spread across the faces of Rex's future active brothers. The atmosphere was gloomy at best. Rex looked dejectedly at the floor. He stared there for a minute or so as condolences were offered, reluctantly. Knowing Rex, I could tell he was thinking. Deeply. Everyone knew he didn't want to let these good brothers down. Then he raised his head, looking at his brothers with a glimmer of hope, and said, "I have an idea. I could rent a U-Haul van and we could all get in the back of it. That way there won't be any cars to draw attention to us. We'll just back the van down the driveway, and we'll all empty out into the house where we'll have Peaches, and beer, and food, and brotherhood all lined up for us."

I'm paraphrasing a little on this, but you get the idea; and so did all the fraternity brothers in the lunchroom at 51 North Wolcott on that warm, optimistic spring afternoon. Rex said he would find out the cost of a U-Haul van that might hold about thirty brothers, but no one seemed to care about what it might cost. "Do it," they said. Almost in unison.

TWENTY-NINE

Lakers and Celtics

BROTHERS IN OUR frat house tended to line up as right- or left-wingers politically, with some in the middle, and some not thinking politically at all. I might have been in this last category, mostly accepting of everyone and their political views. But when it came to sports, particularly team sports played in front of lots of people, there were no in-betweens for me. It was so simple. Like choosing between good and evil. If you were a Lakers fan, for instance, anyone who rooted for the Celtics was just wrong. Misguided. Prone to criminal behavior. Evil in other words. I cheered for the Celtics back in the '60s, and so Lakers fans were all of the above. I mean, how could anyone actually see anything good about a team who paid homage to the devil? It was obvious to everyone except a fan for the other team.

As an illustration, the Celtics had guys like Bob Cousy, Sam Jones, Casey Jones and my all-time favorite player, Bill Russell. Good guys from head to toe. There was a reason these teams, with meager 6'9" Russell at center, won eleven championships in thirteen years. Teamwork. Contrast that with, say, the selfish play of the Lakers, who had guys like Jerry West, Elgin

Baylor, Gail Goodrich and Captain Ming (from *Flash Gordon*) disguised as seven-foot Wilt Chamberlain. See what I mean? Good vs. Evil.

I see things differently today. I know that becoming a fan of anything can, sooner or later, lead one to suspend all aspects of common sense and reason. That's what I can say now, after a career in sports marketing, but I couldn't even come close to admitting that way back in the days of those fabulous Celtics-Lakers championship matchups. To this day I understand why people paint their faces and wear the same underwear for weeks, to ensure their beloved teams win important, potentially seismic, coma-inducing games. I actually did paint some sideburns on my face for a mock Lakers-Celtics seven-game season we played at a local gym, but that's as far as I ever went. Trust me on this.

As a group of sports fanatics, we should have been more understanding when poor frat brother David Partenheimer, a rocket scientist today for sure, walked behind about 20 of us on the couches in the frat house living room during Super Bowl II and asked, "Who's playing?" Please forgive us, David, for that particularly un-brotherly-like response. I can't even remember who played in that game. Neither can 99 percent of the rest of the world. It really didn't matter, did it? You, my friend, had perspective while we didn't. I read once that Michael Jordan would have had to play basketball another 40 years, and make the same amount of money he made when he retired, including all his endorsements in order to have the same net worth as Bill Gates had at that moment. Perspective is important, even if it comes a little late.

But every year, when the World Series, the Super Bowl, the NCAA Final Four, or the NBA Finals came around, a bunch of frat members would forget about being brothers (and just about everything else) while we watched life-altering games being played on the television set in our big, spacious living room. The living room, by the way, had enough yardage so brothers could stomp around behind the couches and chairs assembled in front of the TV, shouting at the referees, the players, the crowd, and ultimately at each other.

Arguments ensued. They weren't personal, of course. Not at first. But they were moving in that direction. We didn't invent trash talking. But we may have added a new dimension to it, by extending our discussions throughout the days leading up to a big game during lunch at the house, dinner at Snappy's Burgers, or pre-game drinks for some at the Joker Lounge.

Some of these games were tape-delayed during this era so people could watch a beloved prime-time scripted show, like *The Beverly Hillbillies* or *Mission: Impossible*, but that didn't matter. Of course, my class schedule was always arranged to accommodate how much I might learn watching an important game. Even our adorable Dream Girl, who we could always count on, didn't show up as often. Cookies or a birthday cake didn't carry the same weight now that we had our game faces on.

What I haven't mentioned is that these games, especially a seven-game NBA Championship series, gave us something to do during the late spring or early summer, when school was all but over for the year, and even the sororities were winding down all their social activities. The campus was emptying out and all the pretty girls in the universe were headed somewhere else, to get suntans and meet boys on beaches. Putting that out of our minds was a good thing. Especially when Good was lining up to play against Evil.

The other thing I liked is that the neighbors couldn't take as many incriminating pictures of the frat house with empty kegs on the front steps or guys sleeping on the roof. The raucous noise emanating from the living room as guys hollered for their team was a disturbance, but one they couldn't really do anything about.

In 1969, the Celtics and Lakers faced off in another classic series. About twenty of us, mostly living in the house, squared off too. At first things seemed to go okay. But as referees missed calls, and players began to inflict physical pain on other players, we also became less gentlemanly. More wrapped up in what was happening on the court. More likely to paint our faces with our favorite team's colors, or consider wearing the same stuff over an extended period of time. More likely to chastise our misguided brothers cheering for Satan.

Eventually the hostility in the living room escalated enough that Celtics fans started watching the games in someone's room, crowding around an even smaller TV but away from the sinister guys on the other side of Good and Evil. Lakers fans started doing the same thing. But unlike what we might have hoped, the trash talking didn't deescalate. We Celtics fans started making appearances in the other's room, briefly opening the door to make a point about the brilliant play of our team. The Lakers fans, sitting down the hall, returned the favor.

Spitballs and paper airplanes, made from college exam sheets, became weapons. And eventually, as the games progressed and became more intense, we began dousing each other with cups of water to cool things off a little. How do you top that, we all wondered, until one night as the series was drawing near its inevitable finale, someone (probably a Lakers fan) had the brilliant idea to use the fire extinguisher hanging in the hall to punctuate his team's loss.

That's when we decided to don our team's favorite colors, and play a seven-game Championship series of our own at the local gym, which had several full courts just waiting for us.

In the actual series, the one that inspired us to mimic our heroes in real life, the Celtics beat the Lakers. So everything was right in the universe. Plus, it went down as one of the great Championship series of all time. What I liked most was that the Celtics weren't even supposed to be there. They finished fourth in the Eastern Conference, losing their last game of the season by 40 points. The Lakers were loaded that year with Jerry West, Elgin Baylor and Wilt Chamberlain, and looked like shoe-ins for the title. The series went seven games like this: The Lakers won the first two by a total of eight points. The Celtics took the next two games by a total of four points. The Lakers dominated the Celtics in Game Five, but the Celtics won the next two games. The last one was played in Los Angeles. Jerry West scored 42 points but it wasn't enough. The Celtics won Game Seven in the last seconds when Don Nelson, who now evidently owns a marijuana farm in Hawaii, took a desperation shot from somewhere near the foul line and missed. But the ball shot off the back rim straight into the air and dropped through the net.

The Celtics hurried off the court, but Bill Russell sought out Jerry West and put his arms around him, consoling the person who would become the first MVP of an NBA series, and to this day the only MVP ever selected from the losing team. Sam Jones and Bill Russell retired that day, the day that the Celtics became the winningest sports franchise in history.

I can't remember anything about our games. Or who won. But the pre-game locker room ritual that took place in the living room of the frat house was classic. So was the warmup drill we all did at the local public gym, just like they do in the big leagues, only in front of maybe ten or so sideline spectators who mostly seemed amused but not impressed. That's because we probably looked homeless dressed in our Lakers purple or Celtics green. Since team jerseys weren't available to fans yet, tie-dye shirts, ragged cutoffs and vintage Converse shoes were prevalent game-day gear. To enhance things, we each chose a player from our favorite team and came as close as we could to looking like him. I wanted to be John Havlicek, but he looked too much like a regular guy who might drive a school bus or could have lived in a frat house. Instead, I chose Emmet Bryant, a role player but who wore very recognizable sideburns that surrounded most of the landscape on his face. Since facial hair wasn't my strength, I resorted to creating his sideburns with shoe polish. I think it took almost a can of it to get the job done. Lanky frat brother Brent Gold imitating Bill Russell, with his stylish goatee, used the rest of my shoe polish on his chin.

The games were competitive and fun, despite the shoe polish that started to run down my sweaty face. We had to end the series, though, when pledge brother Don Pugh, a Laker on this particular day, broke his leg somewhere around Game Four. I remember all of us carrying him off the court and out the doors on the way to the hospital. If only the real Bill Russell would have been there. I know he would have given him a hug.

THIRTY

Rove and Chill

KARL ROVE AND Craig Childers weren't "chill." Just the opposite, in fact. Men with plans. Big plans. Karl moved into the frat house on 51 North Wolcott somewhere around the summer of 1969. We were just a stop along the way. Along the way to the White House, more or less. He even told me that when I first met him. He had unloaded a car full of books and a few t-shirts, I think, into the room just above the frat house lobby. It was one of the biggest rooms in the house and had a large window that looked out over the street, right across from the neighbors who took pictures of our front porch occasionally. He needed a big room so he could stack up all his books in piles, most of them about waist high. They seemed to fill up the room completely, perhaps because my room was pretty empty of books at the time.

I sat across from him and we got acquainted. I was living in the house too, so I wanted to meet our newest housemate. After a while, I asked him what he wanted to do in life. Without any hesitation, he said, "I want to be Chairman of the National Republican Party." And he said it just about that fast. He had a plan, definitely. At the moment, my goal was to figure out what

I was going to do on this nice, warm early summer morning, and maybe stroll over to the Registrar's Office on campus to see how close I was getting to graduating. We were living in different worlds, obviously. Most of the other brothers in the house resided somewhere in between the two of us when it came to goals.

Karl was a skinny, bespectacled kid weighing in around 120 lbs. Like me. That's pretty much where the similarities between the two of us ended. He was extremely bright. Gifted. Focused. Determined. All good things I admired about him. Over time, I also became a little more focused, and I likewise was determined to make my own mark the best I could in the world around me. He certainly made his.

Craig Childers seemed to come out of nowhere, too. One day he was in the fraternity, hanging out and going to school, and one day he was gone. Craig's ceremonial robe is the one that caught fire during Ingress Week when he stood too close to a candle. He was an active member, helping preside at one part of our pledges' graduation ceremony. Mostly girls used candles, and I think guys like us struggled to make them work, so we used them very sparingly. Luckily, the house didn't burn down that night, although it would later for different reasons. And fortunate, too, that someone noticed Craig's smoldering robe and was able to stamp it out before it warmed up his leg too much. Or the rest of the house.

The thing Craig and Karl had in common, besides pretty good intellects and a drive to succeed, was the room on the second floor of the frat house. First Craig had it, and then when he left for law school and a career in Texas, Karl moved in. Or vice versa. Both of them were a little enigmatic. Though friendly and brotherly, you sensed they had a higher purpose all carved out for themselves, sort of like Gordy Gee who lived in the house at one time too, and who later became the president of Ohio State University and then West Virginia University. I wouldn't say these guys were out of my league, although they might. I just think we were on different parallels in the universe.

I had a chance to know Craig a little better than Karl. He was a trivia whiz like no one I had ever met. And he took advantage of that knowledge all summer long, because a local radio station aired a sports trivia contest every night, and the first caller with the correct answer received a free 16" pizza. We figured the pizza could be split among the leftover brothers who lived in the house during the summer. I think there were about eight of us, depending on the day. Some nights Craig was a little hungrier than other nights, and had more of a propensity not to share. We understood this, of course. After all, he was the bread winner, not us. But the problem for Craig was that he couldn't keep using his real name every time he wanted a pizza. The radio station was on to him. So he resorted to using our names from time to time, and he even had to have us make the phone call as soon as he whispered the correct answer into our ears. Then we had to intercept the pizza at some unknowing neighbor's house. Naturally, we started to feel a little entitled.

One night we positioned a ladder below his bedroom window and had one of the brothers tell him he had a phone call down in the lobby's phone booth. The pizza that night seemed especially tasty. Craig forgave us, but not until a little later in the week, as soon as he won another pizza. It probably didn't help that we ate the whole pizza that night without him.

Interestingly, the frat house just had one phone that we placed inside the phone booth between the front lobby and the kitchen. Pledges were supposed to answer the phone a certain way, all professional-like, except in the summer when no one was around. Then sometimes we just let it ring. Karl Rove, however, used the phone all the time. A couple of times, brothers had to almost physically remove him from the phone booth in order to use the phone themselves. Karl had a lot going on that summer.

Karl Rove went on to become world-famous, as you probably know. He was a mastermind for the Republican Party, just like he said he would be. More or less, it looked like he ran the White House, standing right next to President Bush throughout his administration, like a vice president. He was flying all over the world, making speeches and appearing on all kinds of national and worldwide news programs. I think he still does that, and I hear he gets paid thousands and thousands of dollars every time he opens his mouth. I think he read all of those books stacked up in his bedroom in the frat house, and more. Like I said. Brilliant guy. Gifted. Motivated. Driven, in fact. He probably doesn't remember much about living in the frat house that summer. It was just a stop along the way.

THIRTY-ONE

Disneyland

INSIDE FORT KNOX, the Army base where I did my Advanced Infantry Training (AIT), is where they supposedly keep just about all of the gold in the world. That's what some people have said, anyway. Maybe that's just a legend. Before I went there, I watched Sean Connery in my favorite James Bond movie, *Goldfinger*. Goldfinger's plan was to nuke the gold inside Fort Knox, thus making the gold he had personally hoarded incredibly valuable. A brilliant idea, on paper. The movie was made in 1964, so I wasn't sure just how accurate it was about the gold when I got there a few years later. But several of my fellow soldiers said that yes, the gold was there; and the way they kept people from trying to steal it or even looking at it was by placing a big fence around it with a sign that simply said, "DO NOT STEP BEYOND THIS POINT OR YOU WILL BE SHOT." And no one did, at least not until Goldfinger broke into Fort Knox and was thwarted by James Bond. As a former marketing guy, I think the sign the Army was rumored to have made would have been pretty effective at keeping people away from the gold; a pretty good example of a "direct sell."

"Disneyland" is the nickname of the barracks I lived in

at Fort Knox, positioned quite some distance from the gold depository. It was massive. It probably had twenty different barracks buildings housing over two thousand soldiers. The reason it was called Disneyland was that it was brand-new. Everything was built first-class, state of the art, including the toilets all lined up in a long row, similar to the ones at Fort Lewis, only very new and shiny. Except they were still white porcelain, not gold, like you might have hoped or envisioned. Of course, the term "Disneyland" was an anachronism. I was still in the Army, wearing green fatigues and a metal pot on my head to deflect bullets, and crawling around on the ground with a rifle, only this time the ground was frozen solid and occasionally covered with a little snow instead of the mud that was so prevalent at Fort Lewis. I liked the hard ground and a skiff of snow a lot more, at first. By the end of my training it was a toss-up between crawling in snow or crawling in mud. Crawling around in the dirt seemed like a better idea, but then I remembered that when I did that at Camp Roberts and Fort Irwin in Death Valley, it was over 100 degrees. At the end of the day, none of the choices seemed very good. I wondered why the Army always seemed to pick the very worst places to put military bases.

Things are relative, though, and I learned not to complain about my plight one day when I was standing in the chow line headed into the massive kitchen, which for some reason was called the Mess Hall. The guy standing next to me was from Arizona. He was short, like me. I liked him right away. I was mumbling about the chances liver would be served for lunch when he said, "I love the Army. I love every minute of it. Before the Army, I'd never had even one good meal a day. Having three square meals, even if one of them is liver, is fantastic. Having a place to sleep at night is fantastic. Having clothes given to me is fantastic. Having classes about becoming a soldier is fantastic.

I couldn't be happier." I can't say that conversation changed my view of military life completely, but I realized how much things really are relative, and that maybe it was time to start looking at things—especially things in the Army—with a little different perspective. I'm grateful for that conversation, and have remembered it ever since. It was the last time I saw the soldier from Arizona, but I hope he is a general somewhere in the military today, or maybe even a retired general playing some golf in Arizona.

Another memory from the barracks at Disneyland is of Bill Lynch. Bill was from Chicago. He was a handsome guy with short, buzzed red hair, and a good smile. He had signed up for OCS, which is Officer Candidate School. He wanted to be a lieutenant after he finished AIT and OCS. Bill didn't like the Army, though. He wanted out as fast as he could get out. The Army expects you to make a commitment for a lot of years if you become an officer, and Bill didn't want to do that. So, right in the middle of our AIT he told the Army he was resigning from OCS. He just wanted to complete his training and serve somewhere for as long as he had committed. A couple of others in our unit did the same thing. So, guess what the Army did? They sent all those guys straight over to Vietnam. I saw the look in Bill's eyes when he got the notice he was going over there as soon as AIT was over. We became friends in the barracks at Disneyland and in the field where we received our training. I never saw him again after saying goodbye one day, when I was headed home and he was headed to fight the Viet Cong. Even though I was only going to be a soldier on the weekends for the foreseeable future, it was a sad day. A couple of years later, I tried to find him but never could. I hope he's in Arizona, too, playing a little golf and enjoying life.

One of the challenges of AIT at Fort Knox was the weather. It was January and very cold in Kentucky. The Kentucky Derby is held in the spring for a reason. Of course, what the Army does—besides schedule liver for dinner when you are really, really hungry—is find the coldest week of the year to send you into the field for a couple of weeks. It's called "bivouac," and it means in this instance that we'd be sleeping in two-man tents in zero-degree weather, then spend the day crawling around in the snow cradling a rifle. This is probably when I decided never to go hunting with friends, even the best of friends. It was so cold that the Army, in an act of good faith, filled big, empty oil drums full of firewood, letting them burn from about 6 am until it was time for breakfast, flames and dark smoke billowing into the air long before the word "pollution" was heard of.

At first, I wanted to make sure I was up early enough to find a space around one of the drums so I could warm up my clothes, and especially my boots. Soon I discovered that you really didn't need to worry about finding space, because most likely the guy who was already there, standing inches from the flaming receptacle, might burn a hole in his combat boots as he alternately placed each toe on the side of the barrel, forgetting that his toes might be numb from wearing his boots all night. He was probably the guy who didn't listen completely when the platoon leader said to make sure you took your boots off at night so you wouldn't get frostbite. I think we averaged about two guys a day, at least, who had to be hauled off, most likely with frostbite and maybe a couple of holes in their soles to boot.

My problem wasn't my boots; although you should just try sometime taking off your clothes, down to your long johns, with a guy sitting next to you in a small pup tent, juggling your air mattress the whole time and watching to make sure you didn't violate his space, or somehow knock over the small container of "canned heat" that lit up the tent enough for you to see what a mess you were really in. If the enemy was out there, this was precisely the time to attack. Just after sundown when guys were wrestling inside their tents without most of their clothes on, and without complete knowledge of where their rifle might be either. Not to mention the little containers of canned heat lighting up the battlefield all around you. It might be the genesis of the phrase "catching someone with their pants down," militarily speaking.

No, my problem was my air mattress. It leaked. Today you might call it a "smart" mattress, because it leaked slowly. Just slow enough that it was almost impossible to find the leak, but fast enough that around 3 am every morning, I hit bottom. With no air between me and the tarp laid carefully over the snow and ice, it was a wakeup call I can't describe. You would have needed to be there to know how it felt, sharper and much colder than a shower during Ingress Week at the Pi Kapp house. By a long way. At this point, after levitating to some degree, I rotated over and began blowing air back into the smart mattress the Army had issued me, knowing I only had a couple more hours before we were awakened, either by the noise only a trumpet can make if it's not being played by Miles Davis, or by some other guy who they picked because of his shrill, high decibel voice that emanated fiercely throughout the campground.

So now everything was played out in reverse in our two-man tent. Instead of trying to shed our clothes, we were busy trying to find them, making sure we put on the right pants and the Army shirt with your name on it, not the other guy's. Then we crawled out of our tent wearing our boots and helmets and carrying our rifles, headed for barrels full of flaming firewood. It was probably about 4 degrees by my calculations.

And that's how our day began. Every day. It ended the same way. In between all this morning and evening bedlam, we marched or crawled around a lot, but mostly we sat outdoors on hills with makeshift bleachers and a podium with a sergeant who looked like he had slept in a nice, warm bed the night before, and had probably got up just in time to come to teach our class. You could tell because his uniform was all starched up, and his pants had a fine crease from his waistline all the way to the boots where they were inserted. That would take some time to do, I thought.

By now it was usually a little warmer, especially on the occasional sunny day, and all that heavy gear plus the steel pot helmet felt even heavier. Making up for all the missed sleep on my mattress the night before started to get the best of me. I, along with some of my fellow privates sitting on the hill, dozed off. This was okay until the day I lost consciousness, my head jerking backwards just long enough for my steel pot to come off and roll down the sidelines of the bleacher almost to the front row of the class. Unfortunately, I had the last seat on the aisle of the 10th row, and it was a clear path from that point to the podium. It seemed like it took five minutes for my pot to roll down the aisle, all the time making a crunching sound as it picked up momentum. No one reached out to rescue my steel pot. Maybe that's because it was offering a distinct diversion from the lecture by the drill sergeant on the podium. Comic relief was always welcome among soldiers.

A couple of things you should know about the steel pot if you haven't ever worn one. First, they are heavy, and I spent some amount of time trying to balance it on my head and shoulders each day. Secondly, it makes a very distinctive sound as it crashes to the ground. Finally, you should know that they are a lighter green, unlike the helmet which is a dark brown color. If you are sitting in the bleachers with more than fifty guys all wearing their pots, it's obvious if you aren't. There's really nowhere to run or hide. Even on the aisle seat near the back of the class.

The drill instructor, standing on the podium with a pointer and a big map behind him, couldn't help noticing the one guy in his class who didn't have an olive-green metal pot on top of his helmet. Soon I was standing at attention while he talked to me a bit about being a true soldier who understood the importance of the metal pot, as well as the importance of being awake in his very stimulating class that might someday save my life, if I were listening. To help me stay awake for the rest of the class, he had me stand at attention, which was probably a pretty good idea from his point of view. He also had me hold my rifle around the barrel and raise it, stiff-armed, so it was perpendicular to my body. I was alright with that initially, understanding the need to be penitent. But soon the fact that it weighed over nine pounds without bullets started to weigh on me. And my arm. I remember being able to do a lot of pullups in high school, but this was an entirely different exercise.

I don't think I set any military record for holding a weapon on a perpendicular plane to my body. In time, and I think it was a pretty good amount of time, I resorted to opening up my thigh and pointing my boot toe (which I hadn't burned off at the ceremonial barrel activity that morning) so that it could hold the stock of my weapon upright. Eventually the drill instructor showed some mercy and had me sit back down. Someone returned my pot which I wore the rest of the day, proudly, and without any further incident. He did make note of my name, though, and I wondered if it might have been a good idea to put on my bunkmate's shirt that morning when we scrambled to get dressed.

Brian Swinton, SMC, conducts a Chapter meeting.
I'm on the far left, enlisting brothers for a Rush Party.

Special Forces Boot Camp: Erv, Rex center row, gritting their teeth.
Tom Woolf just behind them.

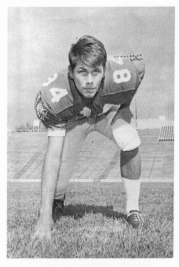

Scott "Hondo" Welling, already
looking like an attorney, even
before he became a PIKE.

JR "110%" Knight. A wide-
receiver (and then some) for
the university.

"U Haul" Johnson and "Bus"
Seldin testing some fishing hooks.

Jon "The Heat" Lervig (left)
with Walt Hanni, heading
north…to Alaska.

Mr. Adventure. From the Alaskan Bush
to the jungles of Cambodia.

Rex (left) and Erv. Best friends from day one.
I can't believe they sat still long enough to become Pi Kapps.

Active duty at Ft. Lewis. That's me on the front row, third from right.
I wasn't able to blend in this much during training, though.

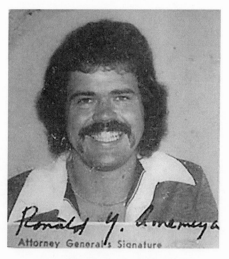

Richard "Fast Eddie" Edwards.
The ultimate concierge.

The brothers gear up for the Bowery at the Old Mill.

Graduation day at the Pi Kapp House, like it or not.
First row, from left: me, Andy, Willard Morris, Dan Paxton.
Top row: Bryce Wade, Pat Roylance, Scott Miller and Craig Childers.

Pat and Marilyn Roylance in love in DC.
These were the best of times.

Erv and Linda Terry, Mr. and Mrs. Adventure.

Lew "Buddha" Bautista and his bride, Leslie about to launch
their first restaurant. I helped out in the kitchen if they needed me.

Me, Steve Bushnell and Lanny Smith with Steve's dad in Mazatlán.
They were already millionaires by now.

Rex "U-Haul" Johnson today. Engineer of the greatest "sneak" in fraternity history worldwide.

THIRTY-TWO

Nordy

STANDING ABOUT 5'10" with a soft body compared to most athletes these days, you wouldn't think John Nordquist could have been an All-American high school quarterback, or a star on his basketball team, or earned a scholarship to play baseball for the University of Utah. But he did all of the above. All of it. He never got injured. He didn't look especially athletic and muscular because I don't think he ever trained or worked out. He didn't need to. He had enough natural ability that he just excelled at whatever game he was playing at the moment. It was just what he did. With a smile on his face. He was easy-going. Kind. Gentlemanly. And a good frat man.

What made him an especially potent baseball player is that he could throw a fastball and a bunch of other pitches right across home plate from the pitcher's mound with either his left or right arm. And impressively, he could sign his name with both hands, starting at opposite ends, writing his signature towards the middle until the letters met!

"Nordy" was also the life of just about any of our world-famous fraternity parties whenever we could coax him to sign his name or throw imaginary baseballs across the living room in front of a crowd. Which wasn't very often. John had watched hundreds of training films of himself throwing a baseball as he sat in the coaches' offices at the university. Videotape wasn't around yet; it was just film in the late '60s, so once the film ran, the coaches simply played it in reverse so they could watch it again from the start. Nordy's mind always worked in unique and unusual ways, and after watching his pitching technique forwards and backwards, he became intrigued with the backwards part of it. Over time, he perfected it on the front steps of the frat house as he demonstrated his classic pitch forwards . . . and backwards. At about three-quarters speed too, so you could be sure to see all the minute details that went into the toss. And the rewind.

He started like you might see any professional pitcher begin, hunched over, foot on the imaginary mound, looking dead serious into the eyes of the imaginary catcher sitting across the way with his imaginary catcher's mitt in position. Face mask on. John even shook his head disapprovingly at imaginary pitches until he finally nodded, signaling when he saw the one he liked and that he was ready. Then came the slow windup, the imaginary glove coming back with the imaginary ball settling in around his chest. He looked right and left, just in case there were runners on the imaginary bases who might think they were smart enough to steal second, or heaven forbid home plate. Then the throw, starting with him raising the glove and ball over his head as his body torqued into position. Finally came the release and the follow-through. Then he paused, holding his position. But he wasn't done. Now imagine what you just saw happen again. Only *backwards*!

Picture the ball coming back to his hand, the hand imitating exactly the toss with just as much oomph and power as the release, the ball and glove working harmoniously with the body in full motion, everything ending up exactly as it started, with the pitcher back in the starting position, nodding and then waving his head in disapproval at the catcher, probably in the 7th game of the World Series. If there was ever poetry in motion, this was it. Perfection, from start to finish to start. Like watching a Rembrandt being created in front of your eyes, almost.

Wisely, Nordquist was careful about displaying his artistic talent. He shyly refused our pleas more often than he submitted to them. It was special to watch because you weren't sure if Nordy might one day say, "I'm retired."

Never big on getting attention, I could see why Nordy was the reluctant showman. It was such a natural, second-nature kind of thing to him that I don't think he thought much about what a hit he was around the house. Or cared about it.

Hondo, our PIKE brother who lived at the front of the house and studied most of the day in his blue bathrobe, was good friends with Nordy. They just clicked, you might say, even though they didn't always share the same perspective about some aspects of life. Hondo was philosophical, studious and intellectual as he prepared to go to law school. Nordy not so much. Nordy was absorbed in the moment. Hondo took the long view. Their friendship, though unexpected, is firm to this day.

One day as I drove back from campus to the frat house, I spotted Nordquist's green and white sedan meandering along the road by the golf course on the east side of campus. We were about a block from the house when Nordy pulled his car over to the side of the road and Hondo got out. Nordy drove on. I suspected they'd had an argument about something. Probably politics. I pulled over and offered Hondo a ride. "What's up with you guys?" I asked him. "Nothing. No problem," he answered, nonchalantly. "It's just that we left campus about thirty minutes ago and the crazy guy just keeps driving along, talking and going nowhere. I gotta get back to studying, and the way things were going, I figured I could walk home faster than Nordy could drive, even though we live just around this corner." Life in the moment. Or life in the future. In simple 30-minute increments. That's what it came down to for Nordy and Hondo. One summer, my father asked if any of my fraternity brothers would be interested in driving a moving van to Chicago to pick up some furniture from an office building and bring it back. I asked Nordy and Hondo, as long as Hondo would drive.

My room was at the back of the house, in the corner. I picked it so I could study without interruption, before I realized that you would be interrupted no matter where in the house you lived. Nordy had the room next door. I always thought girls weren't a big part of his world because he was such a good jock. He was also good at hanging out with the brothers and throwing imaginary baseballs from time to time. Something had to take a back seat. But that all changed when he started hanging out with a girl he met, probably in a phys-ed class. In the second part of his fraternity life, she became a teammate, you might say; and based on the giggles I occasionally heard seeping through the walls (maybe he was demonstrating his backwards pitch for her), she was a good find. Even though they didn't marry, she probably had a lot to do with preparing him for the woman he would marry someday.

A couple of years later, we were surprised when he learned to speak Korean and took a job teaching school in South Korea, and even more surprised when we heard about his marriage. And then his being recruited by the CIA or some similar government agency. I have no idea how a jock from a small community in my home state made it all the way through the

Pi Kapp house to South Korea, got married, and ended up doing some kind of CIA-type secretive work he never talked about. A side job being a spy for the government? Nordy was apolitical. Maybe that's why someone selected him to serve his country undercover. My guess is he didn't have to take a driving test before they hired him.

THIRTY-THREE

The Sneak, Part IV

ON FRIDAY AFTERNOON of "Peach Days," I sat on the front porch of the frat house with C-Note Anderson, and we visited. In front of us, on the street at 51 North Wolcott, was a medium-sized U-Haul van Rex had rented with a plethoric fund graciously donated by about thirty fraternity brothers, who were starting to assemble in anticipation of the party. It was scheduled to start around 3 pm at Rex's wonderful friend's parents' home some blocks away in the Avenues neighborhood.

It had been a nice, warm day, all day, and it looked like it would continue on into the night, almost balmy but not quite. Still spring. But summer was coming, and the brothers were in a celebratory mood. The back door of the van was open, and it looked like it had plenty of room for them, and maybe a little to spare. Some of the brothers glanced into the back of the van, perhaps thinking that it wouldn't be too bad being there for the short ride through the Avenues to the party house.

I honestly can't remember the name of even one brother who climbed up into the bed of that van, nor would I release their names if I could. Except Phil, who left work early and brought his boss from the local bank where he worked part-time. As he helped him into the van, Rex—knowing he wasn't a member of the fraternity—ominously but matter-of-factly said, "I wouldn't bring him if I were you."

Phil responded, "It's okay as long as we're back by 6 pm to close the bank."

Rex responded again with, "I wouldn't bring him if I were you." But Phil wasn't paying attention at this point.

The rest of the men of Pi Kappa Alpha, who had funded this whole event with what may have been enough money to pay for tuition that quarter, were relaxed and very brotherly as they helped each other find a comfortable spot inside. It was about this time that C-Note leaned over to me and quietly said, just about the time Rex jumped into the cab, "You're not going?"

"No," I said.

"Good."

That's all he said. "Good." When I asked him why he wasn't going, he looked at me dead on and chuckled, the same chuckle he always made when he knew something you didn't. I can still see it, but it's hard to describe. It was sort of a chuckle that inflated his cheeks but didn't really emerge from his mouth. I'm sure that chuckle still resides in his repertoire of responses today.

I'll have to piece together what happened next using fragments of stories from various participants who were headed to see "Peaches" that day. It goes something like this:

- Rex drives the van through the neighborhood up to the T Street Market.

- Most of the occupants unload to stock up on snacks and additional drinks.

- When everyone is back on board, Rex leaves the store and drives to the neighborhood.

- After about ten minutes, Rex pulls the van over and addresses the partiers.

- Standing behind the van, he tells them they're too noisy.

- He also informs them they are but a few doors away from meeting Peaches.

- He tells them he's closing the door to the van so the neighbors can't see them.

- CLANK, BOOM, CLICK.

Later, someone told me that as soon as the door was shut and latched, darkness surrounding them, a collective light went on in their heads. In a flash of a second, all 26 Pi Kapps realized they had just been locked in the back of a van. They no longer had control of their immediate destinies. They belonged to Rex, who within minutes would aptly earn his forever-going-forward nickname, "U-Haul" Johnson.

So when he announced, "Brothers, this is a sneak," his "sneakees" so to speak already knew. All sorts of additional thoughts quickly surfaced in their minds, as they sat or stood in the back of a U-Haul in complete darkness. "Where is he taking us?" "Can we talk him out of it?" "What about Peaches?" "Where's the money we spent on Peaches?"

Rex continued, answering their concerns in some manner or other: "Brothers, I'm sorry to inform you that there never was a party. I don't know anyone in the Avenues who would be crazy enough to let us have a fraternity party in his parents' house. And most importantly, Peaches does not exist and never did. Instead, we're going on a trip. Together."

"But what about my bank manager?" pleaded Phil. "Just let him off here."

Securing the lock on the back of the van, Rex "U-Haul" Johnson answered, "I told you not to bring him."

THIRTY-FOUR

Snappy's

I T WAS THE closest thing to an annex the Pi Kapp house ever had. We typically didn't spend a lot of time dining on campus, although there was the famous Big Ed's Burger place by the bookstore, and Hires Burgers in midtown. Both had the finest burgers and hotdogs $2 could buy. But we liked the classic diner atmosphere at Snappy's, the kind that people in America everywhere try to replicate to this day. And that's where we went. Its design was simple: one long countertop that curved enough to allow some extra stools as it headed towards the wall by the front door, surrounded by plate glass windows, and about twenty red, twirling, backless bar stools with a traditional black and white backsplash on the walls behind the grill, which in a random way finished off the place. Vats of grease for long, fresh-cut potatoes, and a grill that workers had to scrape off constantly, waited for your order to be deposited on the other side of the counter. It was so popular that people lined up, sometimes even two-deep behind the stools, waiting for the carnivorous consumer in front of them to swallow somewhere in the vicinity of two thousand calories before heading back to the office.

On a scale of 1 to 10, 10 being over-the-top greasy, Snappy's was easily a 12. If you didn't bite into your burger in a hurry, the bun would get soggy. The fries were so greasy, they put them in a plastic basket surrounded with thick wax paper that was drenched to transparency within minutes. You garnished your burger with ketchup, mustard, pickles and onions, your only choices. And you had to have a large Coke in a fantastically huge bottle that the cook pried open with a small bottle opener he kept in the pocket of his apron. He wore all white, just like in the imitation diners you see in movies, right down to the white elongated cap that covered most of his head. There was no other experience like it in town. What put it over the top, if this wasn't enough, was that it really was a diner: *it was open 24 HOURS A DAY, 7 DAYS A WEEK!* There was not a better burger in America at 2 am. Anywhere. This was perfect for us. Because you never knew what time it might be when someone sitting next to you on the porch of the frat house might just query, "Burger?"

Of course, the best time to make a Snappy's run was after finishing a date, where you had tried to impress a certain girl at some fancier restaurant with how little you could eat and how gentlemanly you really were. So, about 2 am or thereabouts. That's when some of the brothers would end up congregating on the front steps of the frat house, knowing that the inside of that cavernous stomach we all seemed to have was still empty, even after eating some other fancy and empty-of-calories cuisine. At that time of night, or morning, actually, Snappy's might only have a half dozen patrons, leaving plenty of space for hungry Pi Kapps with no worries at all until at least 7 am, when less experienced brothers had signed up for a class. Dress at that time was a little more casual, you might say. Not like the business group that frequented the place at noon or even for breakfast. Ordering was a little more difficult at 2 am, too, because you could either go for the burger combo or the more timely but no less caloric breakfast of scrambled eggs, hash browns and sausage. It was cooked in the same grease the burgers were flipped in; and just like the burgers, everything sizzled in front of you, little bubbles of spray seeming to dance over your meal while it was on the grill. Is America a great country or what?

It was early one morning at Snappy's when Bill Souvall and a couple of Pi Kapp brothers borrowed the garbage truck the driver and his companion had left running on the street right in front of the big plate glass windows, so they could grab a quick bite before starting their rounds. The word I got was that they didn't even finish their order, but maybe grabbed their Cokes as they frantically chased after the big, disappearing truck, with someone inside grinding its gears mercilessly as it lumbered up the street, a few paces ahead of their pursuers.

Years later, when the city was becoming more cosmopolitan, a real estate company bought the land underneath Snappy's in order to put up a new bank. But they knew Snappy's was an icon, so they offered to rebuild it a few feet further north and make it twice as big for the same price. That wasn't fine with the owner, though, who probably spent 18 hours a day at the diner. No. Bigger wasn't better. He wanted them to duplicate his highly efficient, not to mention profitable restaurant right down to the last stool, exactly as it was. Exactly. Not one more stool. Not one inch more of counter space. "If it ain't broke, don't fix it," as the phrase goes.

He knew what he had. He had over-the-top success. He knew exactly how to order buns, burgers, potatoes, pickles, and everything else his customers would consume in any given 24 hours, including Sundays on those twenty or so seats that twirled around so easily to let the next person in. It's an entrepreneur's dream, isn't it! Know your customers. Know your product. Know how to order, hire your staff, and prepare for each and every day. So what if a couple of customers waited an extra ten minutes for a seat at the counter? Careful testing had revealed just how long someone would be willing to stand in line, salivating perhaps, for a Snappy's burger, an order of the greasiest fries in America, and the biggest-ever popped-open bottle of Coke. I wish now I would have used his business as a case study for a marketing class I took at the University. A+, not my customary C+, would have been my grade for certain. Of course, I might have gained a few extra pounds from eating all those burgers during my class research project that semester. But I could have used a few pounds to go along with my A+.

My future employer, Larry Miller, who was also a regular at Snappy's although we hadn't yet met, rescued it just before it went into bankruptcy about thirty years later, moving it to his Megaplex Theatre Complex twenty miles south of its downtown location. It was a wonderfully generous gesture. Alas, it just wasn't the same. No one in their right mind could cook a burger like that today without worrying about people keeling over from heart attacks right there on one of those red, twirling stools. Some people even started wondering if McDonald's might shoot less cholesterol into your arteries than Snappy's. It seemed to have run its course as legitimate greasy spoons go. It was a good run, though. A great run, in fact. An A+ run.

THIRTY-FIVE

The Mudigas

IT STARTED AS a joke. The idea was to have an intramural football team made up of cast-offs who were 5'7" or under. Pledge brother John "Nellie" Nelson, who stood at about 5'6", was the guy who dreamed all this up. He was a pretty creative and funny guy. During Goat Week, he was the one who came up with our skit, which got high marks from the Actives at the time. I can only remember it had something to do with nose spray, which John used quite often for a sinus infection he had. Somehow, he could make just about anything funny.

The name "Mudigas" was invented when we were in the military together. Me, Andy, Nellie and Pat Roylance. Since we were all in different companies, we could identify each other in various marching formations by shouting out the code word without giving away our real names. Nellie's idea. Pretty soon those of us on the shorter side of the fraternity roster had signed up. Nellie would be the coach, and you could see him at intramural games, wandering up and down the sidelines in a trench coat, cheering us on and shouting insults at the other team from time to time. This came naturally to him since he had been a cheerleader in high school. No pushover, Nellie won the university's Intramural Wrestling Championship that year in his weight class.

After every game, John would publish a newsletter and pin it to the bulletin board in the game room. The newsletter, several pages long, highlighted the brilliant play of his team, often referring to us as a "highly efficient machine"—only in more descriptive terms, you might say. By now, John had the attention of everyone in the Pi Kapp house. He didn't have to work very hard recruiting players. It helped that John Nordquist, All-American High School quarterback, wanted to play for The Mudigas. He was probably 5'10" but Coach Nellie waived that part of his contract. Soon others wanted to play for our team, too. Future brain surgeon Wally Reichart, an All-State tackle on his high school team, was among them. More heavyweights from the frat house became "Mudigas" posthaste. Our front line, comprised of former jocks who averaged a little more than the allotted 5'7" height, weighed in around 800 pounds. As you can imagine, they were on the whole very well-built, solid guys, crouching in front of the opposing team of students from the Engineering department, for instance, with just one idea, to protect Nordy as he threw long bombs to his receivers from the pocket. I think Nordy could have stayed in that pocket for an hour if he needed to, or maybe longer, while the rest of us ran around helter-skelter to get open for one of his All-American-type passes, with the endzone in sight, waiting for us to cross its threshold and dance around just beyond the goal line.

For offense, we had my buddy Erv Terry, who should have been a running back at my high school. Among others. It was fun to watch them zig-zag through the holes created by our linemen and sprint towards the white chalk stripe mark just ahead.

All-around athlete Rod Shelton also became a running

back and punt returner. One time I watched Rod run a kickoff
from goal line to goal line on the very first play of a game,
with a cigarette dangling from his lips. My guess is that he
wasn't ready for the game to begin while he chatted with his
teammates, and had been having a pre-game smoke near the
other team's goal line. Suddenly, there came the football lofting
toward him, end over end. Without thinking too much about
things, he put the cigarette between his lips, caught and then
calmly cradled the football as he began running, stiff-arming
his way through the other team, a real live cigarette leaving
a small trail of white exhaust behind him, until he partied a
little and tapped some ashes of his cigarette in the other end
zone after scoring. Rod wasn't big on training in those days.
Just playing. He probably thought he could play football and
finish off that cigarette at the same time. Coach Nelson didn't
feel the need to fine him or even chew him out. Instead, he
ran up and down the sidelines like always, waving his arms
and shouting at the other team. As far as we could tell, there
wasn't anything in the rulebook about running back a kickoff
while smoking.

Since I met the 5'7" requirement I was automatically on the
team, along with just about anyone else who wanted to play. I
played wide receiver and defensive back. I loved our team. Our
front line was so big and quick that I felt sorry for whoever
the opposing quarterback was, standing in his pocket knowing
a brain surgeon or some other heavyweight fast-as-lightning
guy would be clamoring for him in a few seconds. The only
comfort their QB had was that, according to the rules, this was
a gentlemanly game of touch football, more or less.

Our frontline made the rest of us defensive backs look like
All-Americans too, because usually we just had to wait around
for a meager and much hurried toss from their QB to float into
our arms, giving us a chance to scamper towards our own goal

line. I think Rod Shelton is the only guy who crossed the goal line with a cigarette hanging loosely from his lips, however.

I don't remember how many teams played in our league. One other team stood out, though, and we would end up playing them in the championship game. They were called the Greek Underground, made up of men who weren't in a fraternity, and probably scorned being in a fraternity a little. They recruited very well, bringing in non-frat guys from all over the universe, apparently. Their line probably weighed about 800 pounds, too. Their running backs were fast like ours, and they had good receivers and punt returners who seemed too serious and dedicated to have a pregame cigarette before the kickoff. We knew it would be a tough game. We heard about them all during the touch football intramural league sponsored by the university. But they had an advantage we didn't know about, until we lined up to play them in the final game: several of their team members had volunteered as refs, and had been at *all* our games, refereeing them and scouting out all our plays, strengths and weaknesses (not that there were many).

In hindsight, we thought it should have been illegal to play for a team and be a referee for your opponents, too. But that's the way it was. So we played. And played hard. It was a good game even though we lost. As time ran out, and they were scoring what I think was the winning touchdown, one of their linemen gave me a badge of honor; his forearm to my chin, splitting it open and sending me to the hospital for about twenty stitches. I still can't grow any whiskers there. I think Erv took me to the hospital, and we lamented over all the "what if" plays and calls. The big "what if" though, was "what if" a team of 5'7" "misfits" had won the Intramural Championship for Pi Kappa Alpha.

THIRTY-SIX

High Crimes and Misdemeanors

TODAY, IT WOULD be a crime to steal a police car. Even if you returned it in perfect condition. In the early Sixties, though, things were a little different. Looser. I think of Barney Fife driving his police car around Mayberry in the popular TV Series *Andy Griffith*, and then I think of the campus police department at the University of Utah in a similar way. So I'm guessing they were just happy to get their patrol car back in one piece, after Tony Polychronis and another Pi Kapp brother borrowed it from a parking lot when it went unattended for a minute, and then drove it all over the campus and a little beyond, taunting the real campus police over the radio they learned to operate soon after turning the keys in the ignition. I think they turned on the flashing bright red and blue lights on top of the car too, but just for a second. Maybe the police department guys weren't too worried. They had another car, after all. And they put it to good use that night to chase down their missing vehicle, which seemed to pop up here and there around campus all evening long. What made it fun was the radio, which they used to give the real police their location, or at least hint about their location. Police HQ had a radio, too, and they kept in touch with car #2, which was now in the race to find Car #1. These two PIKES were very good drivers, especially after taking classes on campus for several years. They knew about some of the little-known nooks and crannies in between buildings where you could temporarily hide a police car. In the spirit of cooperation and *esprit de corps*, the Pi Kapp brothers stayed in touch quite frequently, giving their policeman friends updates over the police radio, saying things like "you're getting warmer" or "you're ice cold" as they listened in to the conversation back and forth among the campus cops. I'm not sure how accurate the updates were, or if the police at HQ trusted our brothers, but things worked out. Further, I doubt the campus police found any pocket change on the front seat to cover the cost of gas for Car #1, which they eventually located, parked along a dark, quiet street in perfect condition.

As far as I know, Pi Kapps haven't spent any time in jails. No reported criminal activity, or even misdemeanors. There was the car accident caused by Rod Shelton when he tried to park on top of Dick Lybert's shiny new Camaro one night in front of the frat house, but that was just a traffic violation of sorts. Pi Kapps were, on the whole, really quite docile and well behaved. Prone to a little good-natured mischief. There was an incident where someone impersonated an auditor and was able to remove one of his brother's parking tickets from the campus police department files, but I think he was a Sigma Chi, not a Pi Kapp who might only borrow a piece of police equipment for a little while.

Just about every fraternity made what they sometimes call "panty raids," which required brothers running through sorority houses at the most inopportune times to gather up underwear that might be laying around in some of the bedrooms. Since I never heard of anyone getting arrested for this, I assume the girls weren't completely upset with the idea.

Two of my more studious brothers took an art class as a diversion from their regular classes in business and psychology. I don't think they knew when they signed up that part of the time they would be painting nude women, who would pose at the front of the class. At least that's what they said. Others from the fraternity tried to enroll in an effort to further their own intellectual development, but it turns out the class was full.

One spring, some of the brothers were especially restless, and pretty soon there were about eight or nine motorcycles parked in front of the house, right on the front lawn. Although I was never a huge fan of motorcycles, they would become a real style statement later, when Harley Davidson made it very macho and cool to have one of their big, big bikes. For now, the brothers drove mid-sized bikes around campus and around town, and maybe up some of the freeways into the nearby mountains.

John Anderson, who became a very successful attorney and tragically died of ALS (Lou Gehrig's disease) some years later, may have been one of the instigators. I rode on the back of some of the brothers' bikes a few times, and my conclusion was that they were death traps. Especially on the streets around town, where about 90 percent of the vehicles were cars, not mid-sized motorcycles with hardly any metal around them for protection if you had to "lay it down."

Once in high school, I had ridden on the back of Lew Bautista's Vespa motorcycle, and we had to lay it down on a busy road when the gears locked up. Suddenly Lew was trying to maneuver the little death trap so it would stay upright. At the time, I had no idea why he was doing all this weaving. I thought he was just screwing around. But pretty soon we tipped over sideways, and the bike took off on its own while Lew and I slid along the asphalt in our cut-off Levi's shorts. I remember standing on the side of the road, looking at my bloodied legs with little rocks embedded in them, holding parts of my shorts in my hand, and chewing out Lew before I knew the real story.

Remembering all this, I stopped riding with my Pi Kapp brothers on the back of their motorcycles that spring, especially after a close call on the back of U-Haul Johnson's bike when a car switched into our lane unannounced. Luckily, we squeezed into the next lane, sharing it with another car. Both drivers looked perturbed at us, like we really had no business putting our motorcycle in their path. That was my last ride. By the time school started next fall, there weren't any motorcycles parked on the front lawn of the Pi Kapp house. Not one. There had been enough close calls by every brother that they decided walking to school was not all that bad of an idea. Maybe they could run through a sorority house on the way home, anyway, helping clean up here and there.

Of all the harmless mischief we created, I never thought dart games, using the little soft rubber tipped arrows you shoot out of plastic guns, would become such a big thing. It started one rainy spring Friday afternoon when C-Note and a couple of others bought them at a novelty store, and then started shooting them around the house at no one in particular. Pretty soon, teams started to form. Future business leaders and chemical engineers, among others, began hiding around the house, while another team crept around looking for them. It was hide-and-seek with flair, and it quickly became serious business. More dart guns appeared. I wondered what people would think if they just showed up at the house, seeing Pi Kapps hiding in the bushes or under the pool table with little plastic guns loaded with rubber-tipped darts. If your girlfriend showed up and saw you hiding in the bushes with a dart gun instead of looking in a physics book, would she wonder what a future with you might really look like, for example? But that didn't stop us. To make the stakes higher, one of the brothers made a flag with a somewhat questionable drawing that became the trophy. When your team wiped out all the other brothers, you received the flag and makeshift flagpole which you could keep until another team dethroned you. I knew things were really serious when brothers started arguing about whether they had been hit with a dart or not. "Flesh wound" or "you just grazed me" were being bantered about as heated discussions ensued.

Running through the hall, one of our brothers (who will go unnamed) jumped to miss an oncoming dart aimed at his legs, but forgot about the casing around the triple-wide, very stationary solid oak door frame separating the lobby area from the living room. This may have been an early instance of the phrase that would become popular years later, "Knock yourself out," which is pretty much what he did. There weren't many official time-outs, but this was one of them. Otherwise, the games continued on throughout the night and extended for the next week or two, around the clock. I realized things were bordering on mania when we had to elect a teammate to actually sleep with the flag in his locked bedroom, cradling it carefully in his arms all night long. If his room didn't lock, he blocked the door with a chair. Perhaps we were losing perspective.

Then things got even crazier, and we threw perspective out the door, when the Sigma Chi's, a well-respected fraternity like ours, jumped into the game. For several weeks, the flag was captured and, under new rules, positioned in the living room of the winning house of the day. The Sigs, as we called them, were pretty good rivals. We didn't like losing to them in intramurals, or having a lower overall GPA than them, and we certainly couldn't accept the idea of having them capture our flag, displaying it in their frat house living room. We took pride in the flag. Someone in our house had made it using a torn shirt and some magic markers. The entire game was our invention. We were the founding fathers. Battle lines had been drawn. This was war.

If the Sigs had the flag, our team resorted to sneaking into their house late at night, camouflaged, perhaps after a run to Snappy's Burgers downtown, to steal it back. And vice versa. Strategic thinking became important. Sometimes we tried to divert the enemy. Enlisting a few sorority girls to visit outside their house, hoping the sound of giggling might entice them to abandon the flag for a minute didn't work. Inviting some of their brothers to a bogus party didn't distract them either. Nor did we fall for their plebian pranks. We were seasoned, well-educated (for the most part) frat men by now. When it was over, we all remained friends. I cannot for the life of me remember who ended up with the flag. Interest waned after a few hard-fought weeks and our minds turned elsewhere. Maybe someone remembered that we were still in school, and there were final exams and class projects to deal with. No one thought for very long, however, about trying to pass off the events of those weeks as a project for a grade at the university. I doubt it would have even earned a C+.

THIRTY-SEVEN

In the Line of Fire

I DIDN'T KNOW WHAT to expect when I joined the Army Reserves in 1966.

My friends and I did it on a whim. In hindsight, like so many other experiences in life, it turned out to be a good thing. I gained an appreciation for what it takes to defend our country. I was a reluctant soldier, and that showed up from time to time as I just tried to get through my Advanced Infantry Training, unconcerned about winning any medals. But there were many who made it their life-calling, and would gladly take a bullet for America. I admired these great men. They are true patriots no matter what is going on in the world around them. All kinds of protests and anti-war demonstrations didn't affect them. My buddies Andy, Pat, Nellie and I were living a dichotomy. We might be watching anti-war protests near the Union Building on the university campus on Friday afternoon, and then get trained to dispel rioters on Saturday, wearing our military gear complete with rifles and bayonets on the Army base.

What was truly sad, however, was what happened when the war was over, and America gave our returning war heroes from Vietnam the cold shoulder. It was hard to watch. Hard to understand. Maybe the country was embarrassed about entering into what turned out to be a terrible, unwinnable war. I remember the last day of the war in Vietnam, watching it unfold on television, as a helicopter literally plucked the remaining soldiers and nurses off the roof of the American Embassy just as the Viet Cong were overrunning it in throngs. It was depressing. But we should have, as a country, given all the soldiers a warm welcome and a huge tickertape parade. Sixty thousand men and women were in the line of fire but never returned. Eventually a beautiful memorial wall was built in Washington, D.C. as a tribute to our fallen soldiers, but we should have done a lot more for the ones who made it back.

At Fort Knox in 1967, the training became more serious, as many of the soldiers in my company began preparing to go to Vietnam still hoping to win the war. Reality hadn't completely sunk in. I only had a few months of active duty left, but my friend Bill Lynch who had opted out of OCS Training would soon leave for 'Nam. He paid more attention in classes than I did, never dozing off and having to stand at attention because his steel pot had come unhinged and rolled to the front of the class.

Our drill sergeants started prepping us for one of the culminating tests in AIT, where we would have to climb out of a bunker and do the low crawl with our M-14 rifles around barbed wire and other obstacles, as bullets were fired over our heads. We did this at night, and the bullets were called "tracers." Tracers looked like long neon tails as they zipped over our heads. Most of these tracers were just like rubber bullets, but some were supposedly real bullets. The drill sergeants warned us that sometimes even the real bullets ran out of gas and fell onto the ground where we were crawling along. Just like in real combat. We were all a little spooked after that lecture. I figured they were joking, because you couldn't be losing any men in training before they ever graduated as real soldiers and went to Vietnam. At the same time, you couldn't help but wonder just a little bit.

However, we had other things to worry about before that happened. Staying awake in the field classes, sitting on a hill with your metal pot over your helmet, was one of them. Getting enough sleep was another, because nighttime in the barracks was sort of like daytime, only noisier. And there was always the issue with food. Next to liver, which 98 percent of us dreaded seeing in the chow line, there were C-rations, the food the army invented out of mostly dust, I think, and then inserted it into little olive-drab tuna-like cans. C-rations is what we ate in the field, because they were pressure-packed with literally no taste whatsoever. A can might be labeled "chicken," but it tasted just like the one that was labeled "beans." And so on. And they were a solid mass like Jell-O. And they tended to stay solid in your stomach for days as you eyed the row of toilets in the latrine, wondering when would be the best time to visit them. Why didn't they invent "A-rations", or even "B-rations"? Why did they have to go to the letter C, knowing that most men would figure out before opening a can that these were not top of the line? They weren't even C+ rations, which I could maybe have accepted.

Maybe the most dreaded day in AIT at the Disneyland barracks, other than the day you might get shot with real tracer bullets, was the day you were assigned to do KP. KP means Kitchen Patrol or Kitchen Police. It's when you have to show up at the kitchen at 3:30 in the morning for duty. You were likely to do dishes, set the tables, and serve liver or other delicacies. And you do it for breakfast, lunch and dinner. Then you clean up everything else and head back to the barracks at about 10 or 11 pm, depending on which job you have. It's almost a 24-hour work day.

At Disneyland, where two thousand soldiers all did drills, they made a special mess hall for meals, which as you might guess was big enough to serve every one of us. I think about 30 or 40 soldiers were on KP at any given time. So I didn't worry too much about being on time that morning, having wrapped a white towel around the end of my bed so some guy could gleefully wake me up. When I arrived at that massive mess hall, the only job left was cleaning pots and pans. And here's why it became problematic. Imagine the chefs cooking up food for two thousand soldiers. Imagine how big the salad bowls would be, or how big the pans were in order to hold two thousand pounds of liver. Even the serving tongs were huge. In fact, the bowls were so big you almost had to crawl into them in order to wash them. The Army took care of that, though, by having three large vats for these behemothic bowls. The first vat contained soap and water. The second one was where you rinsed them, and the third was heated to just below boiling in order to sterilize the pots and pans. The Army thought ahead on this and provided huge grappling hooks, so you could avoid scalding your hands as you dragged the bowls through that particular vat. Then, pulling them out, you rested them on a huge plank for drying and cooling. The chefs were like drill sergeants because they were always yelling at us to get a certain pot or pan ready for them. If we weren't fast enough, sometimes they burned their hands trying to pick up a pot or pan that hadn't been on the drying board very long. Boy, did we hear about that. If the chef was particularly difficult, occasionally we had a tendency to let something stay in the sterilizing vat a little longer. We figured we were going to get shouted at anyway, so why not send him a message at 200 degrees.

By the time the night was over, I thought you should get a special medal to wear on your uniform, or maybe a plaque you could hang in your home, saying you'd survived not only the Army but KP too. It would be an even bigger plaque if you had the unfortunate duty of washing pots and pans for 24 hours at Disneyland.

Luckily, you only did KP once or twice during your stint at Fort Knox, and you tried to keep your head in the game so you wouldn't get an extra tour of duty in the kitchen. The rest of the time you were on maneuvers. On cold, hard, frozen, snow-packed ground. Eating C-rations. The eight weeks of training seemed like 80 weeks. We trudged around, learning about fighting the enemy. And we got ready to crawl along at night, just below the real tracer bullets that might land on your head. I had reasoned everything would be fine that night, and it was. But when you are in a ten-foot-deep bunker looking up at those tracers, they seem to fly just over the top of the ladder leading up to the imaginary battlefield, just barely over your head. We took our turns, waiting in the line to the ladder, watching the bright red- and orange-colored tracers whiz by. When my turn came, I stopped looking at the tracers and hurried up the ladder and onto the ground, scurrying on my stomach toward the finish line. I even turned over on my back once to look at the tracers whiz by. They had to be about 15 feet high, so that even if a soldier panicked and stood up, he wouldn't be in danger.

Through all of this, even though it was drudgery, I would have rather been in a remedial math class at my university on a Friday afternoon with all kinds of girls running around noisily outside. I gained a great respect for the Army. For our country. And for the sacrifices so many would continue to make in order to guarantee our freedoms and ensure that our flag always flew over it, far from any tracer bullets. Despite all the turmoil over the Vietnam War and everything else that was going on, I became convinced I lived in the greatest country in the history of the world.

THIRTY-EIGHT

The Sneak, Part V

C-NOTE ANDERSON AND I lingered on the front porch of the Pi Kapp house after Rex Johnson drove his rented U-Haul van away to find Peaches, with our beloved brothers and a branch manager for a local bank all loaded up in the back of it. Once they disappeared around the corner, with the back door wide open so everyone could see outside, I was able to pry the rest of the details out of him. He was the only brother, other than Rex's pledge mate and future doctor Pat Knibbe, who knew the full story about Peach Days. It was the most brilliant plan I had ever heard of, other than perhaps when the US invaded the Normandy beaches in France on D-Day 1944, something I had learned about in US History 101 way back as a freshman.

A few years later, *The Sting* with Robert Redford and Paul Newman would win seven Academy Awards, but had nothing on Mr. Johnson's own supremely executed deception. In fact, in that movie, even using an elaborate ruse only one man was conned, not the 26 guys Rex convinced to get in the back of a U-Haul van for a party that didn't exist, and for which they had all paid for in advance. Not only did they pay for the party, they paid for their ride in a U-Haul van which Rex had charted to Preston, Idaho!

Andy's chuckle soon turned, along with mine, to outright guffaws and knee slaps as we sat there on the front porch, rethinking what Rex had wrought on all those hapless Pi Kapp brothers and the branch manager of the bank who would probably lose his job. It had to be, hands-down, the greatest sneak in the history of fraternities worldwide.

The two of us figured it would be several hours at least before we heard anything from the group of wayward travelers. Then, after Andy and I reconvened on the porch when the sun was setting behind us, brothers started returning. Slowly, wearily. And angrily. They arrived in taxis, or took a bus, or called a girlfriend, or hitchhiked back to the frat house, just to have the pleasure of announcing Mr. Rex "U-Haul" Johnson's impending demise. More than a few indicated, with the firmness of an employer about to fire a worker who had shamed the organization, that it was over for Rex. *He would not be an Active in this upstanding fraternity. Not a chance. This went way beyond the bonds of fraternal love. This was a disgrace. Far below the most unworthy of Pi Kapp pledges. A pledge worthy of active status would be true to his word and deliver his active brothers to Peaches, the exotic dancer waiting for them at some friend's parents' house in a rich neighborhood, and who wouldn't ever have the audacity to lie to them and take their money a little at a time, over a month or maybe longer, and do it with a straight face the whole time. Who does that guy think he is?* was more or less the diatribe they shared with us.

What Andy and I knew intuitively, of course, was that Rex Johnson would indeed become an active member of Pi Kappa Alpha, and even if Goat Week (or Ingress as it was now called) might be difficult, since all 26 or so members who had taken a ride in that U-Haul van would be hazing Rex to the third degree, he was about to become one of the most famous frat men of all time. If anything, the guys from the back of Rex's U-Haul van should probably disappear during the week instead of hazing Rex. I mean, they bought his story. They took the bait. None of them could probably ever watch *The Sting* when it came out in 1973. It would stir up very painful memories, no doubt. And even if they told the story of what happened that spring day, could they ever actually admit to their children or grandchildren that they had spent some time in the back of Rex's U-Haul van? It was not something to boast about.

What Andy and I didn't know was the rest of the story. Our returning active brothers filled us in. Grudgingly, the occupants told us about the trip to T-Street Market, the stop along the way when Rex was able to close the door and lock them in the van, and his declaration that Peaches was not real. None of it was real, it turned out. Even I, Rex's second-best friend at this point, didn't suspect that Peaches was a fictional character, created in the one and only mind of Rex Johnson. Or that the house in the Avenues didn't exist either. Our good active brothers and the guy that used to work for a bank and his manager had lots of time to mull that over on the way to Preston, Idaho, which calculated at "U-Haul van + 26 men" speed would be several hours.

But inside the van were Pi Kapp geniuses, including future graduates in engineering, business, law, medicine and physics, who would figure out in about an hour how to undo the lock on the back of the van from the inside and open it up. I suspect the air in the van was not as fresh as it was before the doors were locked, and it couldn't have been much of a joy ride in the back, especially in the dark, not knowing whether you were going straight or left or right, or up a hill or down a hill, until a split second before it happened.

Normally, it would have been a big relief to have all that fresh air available to you, except that when they opened up the van from the inside, they found out they were on the main street of a good-sized city, about an hour outside of our town, and all kinds of cars were lined up behind the van at about 5 pm during rush hour, as 26 or so guys came spilling out onto the street, and who mostly crowded around the guy in the cab of the van for some reason, who was stopped at a red light. Soon, many of them were hanging onto the door of the cab of the van, trying to unlock it and pull the guy driving the van out for a good talking-to. The story Andy and I heard was that Rex was trying to bounce them off the side of the van, and also from the windshield where at least one Pi Kapp had positioned himself, by driving helter-skelter down the street, weaving around, hoping to jettison his extremely unruly occupants so he could continue on, perhaps to Preston. Eventually, Rex was removed from the van and sent walking. I'm still unclear about where the van ended up, but it never showed up in front of the Pi Kappa Alpha house again. Pat Knibbe, who had followed the U-Haul van without anyone knowing it, picked up Rex after his active brothers had removed him from the driver's seat and kicked him to the curb. They raced back to the Pi Kapp house and were actually watching from the neighbor's bushes without any of us knowing it, listening to the returning chants of the ill-fated 26.

As the day went on, I kept thinking about a phrase my father used from time to time to tutor me when I looked like I might fall for the latest money-making scheme: "If it sounds too good to be true, then it probably is."

And I remembered C-Note Anderson and the sneak we planned as freshmen, when 26 of us threw a fishing net over an Active who played for the university tennis team during practice, and hauled him away about fifty miles and left him chained up in his skivvies. It was a great sneak. But like any fraternity sneak up to now, we had to overwhelm our target physically, literally dragging him away, a couple of us collecting a bruise or two in the process. We had to pay for the gas to drive him all the way to another city and come back. And then we had to wait for him to verbally unload on us during Ingress Week. We had to endure hearing things like, "So you guys think you're tough. Ten grade schoolers could have done what you did. You guys are wimps, stupid impotent little wimps." Stuff like that. All during Ingress.

But that's not what would happen during Ingress for Rex. Honestly, what could the ill-fated 26 or so active brothers really say to him? They couldn't say he was stupid. They could say he was clever, but that's really not hazing. They could say he lied to them. But what a lie! Just saying that comes out hilariously flat. You'd almost choke on your own words or start laughing uncontrollably when you realized that without you, the sneak would have fallen flat on its face. You had been duped to the 26th power, and you knew it. You had nothing on Rex "U-Haul" Johnson. Those of us who didn't jump in the back of that van that day were all silent allies for Rex. We had his back, so to speak, even if he hadn't had ours. And that's how it played out in Ingress for Rex. He kind of walked through it, albeit on tippy toes. With those bright eyes and tight-lipped smile that made you wonder if you were his best friend, or just the target of his next big con.

1969

We learn how to moonwalk

On the whole, 1969 was a pretty good year, one worth remembering, especially when the USA landed Neil Armstrong on the moon that summer. I remember sitting in my favorite restaurant, the Pizza Oven, with some friends watching it live on television. Close to 650 million others also watched it live on TV that night. It was a big deal. Neil literally bounced off the last rung of the ladder of his spacecraft and said some immortal words he probably dreamed up during his ride from Earth with Buzz Aldrin: "that's one small step for man, one giant leap for mankind." I wonder if he ever had writer's cramp.

Some other pretty good things happened that year, too. The Advanced Research Projects Agency Network (ARPANET) launched what eventually became the internet, by connecting computers in four major universities. Al Gore, who may have claimed to have started the internet, was nowhere in sight when this happened, as far as I know (in August of 1969 he enlisted in the Army after graduating from Harvard).

Four hundred thousand people showed up for Woodstock, the rock concert held on farmland in New York. The Beatles released *Abbey Road* and performed their last public concert, concluding with the hit song, *Let it Be*. The Last weekly edition of *The Saturday Evening Post* was published. A meteorite exploded over New Mexico. The first Jumbo Jet, the 747 went airborne. Golda Meir became the first female Prime Minister of Israel. Next door, Palestine elected Yassar Arafat to run its Country.

Sir Robin Knox-Johnson became the first person to sail around the world without stopping. Boris Spassky was crowned the world's chess champion after a marathon 23 matches. Led Zeppelin pumped out its first album in record time after getting together for a weekend rehearsal. Mario Puzo published *The Godfather*, the X-rated movie *Midnight Cowboy* won an Academy Award for its director John Schlesinger, and Paul Newman and Robert Redford starred in the highly popular bandit buddy movie *Butch Cassidy and the Sundance Kid*.

But still, all wasn't right in America. Charles Manson and his "family" invaded the home of Sharon Tate and brutally murdered her and everyone else in the home at the time. The next day they killed two more people in California, Leno and Rosemary LaBianca. Lieutenant William Calley was charged with killing 109 civilians in Vietnam while on a military patrol with his squadron. And to top it off, the Zodiac Killer shot and killed a taxi driver in San Francisco, supposedly his last murder.

To protest racial inequality, fourteen Black athletes got kicked off the University of Wyoming's football team for wearing black armbands into their coach's office. The first military draft lottery since World War II was held. Three hundred college students stormed the Harvard Administration building in the name of Students for a Democratic Society, resulting in 45 injuries and 184 arrests. *The Brady Bunch* TV series began its five-year run. The first Gap store opened in San Francisco. Willie Mays, who passed away in 2021, became the first baseball player to hit 600 home runs since Babe Ruth. The Mets won the World Series, The Celtics earned their 11th NBA Championship title, and Joe Namath guaranteed his New York Jets would beat the Baltimore Colts in Super Bowl III. And they did.

The Altamont Speedway Free Festival, featuring the Rolling Stones, was organized in California as a follow-up to Woodstock, but turned violent when at least two people were killed by members of the Hell's Angels, who had been hired as security. Some say the concert marked the end of the '60s. Earlier that year, the Stones' founder Brian Jones drowned in his swimming pool. Mary Jo Kopechne tragically drowned too, when a car being driven by Teddy Kennedy fell off the Chappaquiddick Bridge on the way home from a party. Richard M. Nixon was inaugurated as the 37th President of the United States.

Maybe you could say it was a decent year in some respects. But certainly not all. Better than its predecessor. If we consider that one a failure, 1969 probably gets a C+.

THIRTY-NINE

Gym Rats

I GOT HOOKED ON basketball at a young age. In college it became an obsession. I wasn't tall, so I probably should have stuck to golf and tennis. I didn't know I would burn out my knees as well as my hips until years after I graduated. But I loved the game, and the university campus had a great recreation center, with about a half dozen full courts in several different open gyms. You got in free if you had a student card and showed it to a student seated at the desk by the front door. The ticket-taker was often a perky, athletic young girl, which was a bonus. A group of frat brothers started playing there every Saturday morning, from 9 am to noon or beyond. Funny I couldn't make it to class that early. Hard to compare a lecture on statistical analysis with three-on-three pickup basketball.

We played against other students who were also obsessed enough to be there, or we played against each other. Once, after a particularly long stint on the courts, U-Haul Johnson and I ate nine hamburgers (he says it was ten), six orders of french fries, and six mugs of root beer at Hires Big H drive-in downtown. We couldn't possibly have digested that many Snappy's burgers.

It was during a Saturday morning fracas that JR "110%" Knight sprained his ankle. The thing that bothered me, I guess, was that we hadn't played very long, and I didn't see it happen, so I couldn't tell how serious it was. But I wasn't ready for even a couple of burgers from Hires. The games were good that morning. Close. Fairly intense for pickup games. I tried to encourage JR. "Fight through the pain," I said. "Try giving 110%." But he was done. As we walked down the long hall towards the parking lot, JR limping ahead of us, he suddenly collapsed on the floor. I knew JR. I knew he would be fine. I had been tossing footballs at his head to sharpen him up for his games at the university. But the young, athletic-looking girl behind the table near the front door panicked. "Help him," she shouted. "Quick, wrap your t-shirt around his ankle." I had been sauntering out of the gym, dragging my old but relatively priceless t-shirt behind me with the rock group Chicago plastered on the front of it. She probably couldn't perceive its true value at the moment.

"This t-shirt?" I exclaimed. "I just bought this t-shirt. I'm not giving it up for a gimpy ankle." Yes, I lied about just having bought it. And later, when JR was more conscious, I apologized for the lie. But I thought it might do some good for JR if I made a point about the relative unimportance of his ankle when it came to his team. And my beloved t-shirt.

You won the honor of being a gym rat not just by being inside one for an extended period of time, although that was probably the main criteria. You could also be in the weight room, on the tennis court or golf course, shooting hoops on the neighbors' garage rim, or dunking them on the eight-foot basket in the backyard of the fraternity house. Two frat brothers who were consummate gym rats were twins Rob and Rick Folger. They were high school standouts and won plenty of accolades for the hours they spent on the basketball or tennis courts. They won the high school doubles tennis state championship, and Rob was an All-State basketball player for my high school. He seemed to move so rhythmically on the court, launching up deep jump shots with extreme accuracy even with a couple of guys guarding his every move. Rick went on to be a professional tennis coach and teacher, so gym attire was an essential part of his wardrobe, too.

Gym rats don't always look like gym rats, so it's good not to judge them by their appearance. One night my friend and Pi Kapp brother Steve Bushnell and I decided to play some hoops, but we knew the only gym open that late was a good distance away from the university and would be closing soon. To beat the clock, we hurriedly packed some gym clothes and drove to the south side of town. In the locker room, we each pulled out our attire to get dressed. Upon further inspection, it looked like we might have packed without thinking things through. I realized, after donning my attire and looking in the mirror, that this is what would usually be worn on a beach in Hawaii, only with sandals instead of gym shoes. Not gym rat appropriate. Steve didn't look much better, but he made what I thought was a much more critical mistake: he packed two left shoes. Two. Left. Converse basketball shoes. We stood there looking at each other, laughing at our images in the mirror a little, and weighing in on whether to drag ourselves back to the university or stay, seeing if we could fit into a couple of pick-up games out on the court.

I don't know if you've ever worn two left (or right) shoes, but if you have you know how it feels. And if you look at someone who is, they just don't look right. It's hard to put your finger on it, like they are off balance in life generally. One thing for sure, they do *not* look athletic. So when we walked onto the court, the guy with two left feet and the Hawaiian tourist who had wandered into a gym, everyone noticed us right off. Play came to a halt. Collectively they looked at us, not approvingly either. *These guys aren't gym rats*, they seemed to be saying. And then something unexpected happened; almost in unison, several teams pointed in our direction. "We got you guys next," they said.

The fun part of the rest of the night was that we surprised them, not looking like we could play basketball but actually being able to with some degree of proficiency. Steve had that extra-long jump shot he could shoot with extreme accuracy from anywhere outside the locker room, even with two left feet. I liked hoisting up shots, too, and so we were able to win every two-on-two game we played. As the night went on, things got a little heated. We weren't supposed to saunter in and win out. Especially looking like a tourist and a guy with two left feet. That's when some of the players started getting more physical, and one of them violated the unwritten rule of gym etiquette, sliding underneath me when I was in the air, shooting the ball. It's such a no-no that the NBA even has a rule about not doing it. I suffered one of the worst sprained ankles of my life, and had to limp out of the gym in my beach costume with a bag of ice tied to my foot. I understood JR Knight's pain a lot better. On the way out, I told the guy who took away my landing space that he was disqualified as a gym rat and should take up some other activity in life. Anything but sports! I tried to shame him the best way I could.

There wasn't a dress code at the frat house or on campus for that matter, so gym attire was acceptable for most occasions. Especially if you avoided wearing two left shoes. My gym rat buddies and I even wore sweatshirts and sweatpants to one of our brothers' pinnings at a sorority house. We looked at it as a tribute to him if a group of us stood by the piano, wearing our game gear, holding a candle and serenading him as he kissed

his girlfriend and pinned his Pi Kappa Alpha pin delicately on
her dress.

At one point I was able to get a date with the perky, cute and
athletic girl who took tickets at the gym, the one who had tried
to get me to offer up my t-shirt to JR. I tried to tell her the whole
thing was just in fun. We had a few dates for which I never wore
gym clothes, but I think she was looking for someone who she
felt was more loyal and committed, not the guy who seemed
to hang around the gym regularly, playing hoops while she
worked.

FORTY

Then there was The Bowery

THE CLASSIC SONG by Three Dog Night, "Mama Told Me Not to Come," epitomizes the activities that went on at The Bowery, an annual fraternity party that was talked about a lot in the frat house, but never in very much detail. This will be a relatively short chapter, in other words.

I confess that I attended every one of these parties during my tenure at 51 North Wolcott. Everyone did. The idea was *not* to take your favorite girl, because it would be your last date with her. It would be better to go solo, which is what I ended up doing each year, than show up with a girl who had any degree of sophistication and especially morals. About half of us went solo, and half took dates, lining up more or less with the culture of the fraternity. Since most of the guys who took someone didn't plan on having any kind of a long-term relationship with her, we weren't always on our best behavior. After one Bowery, an unnamed frat brother's date had become quite inebriated and a little incoherent, and he ended up carrying her to her front porch, propping her just inside the screen door, and ringing the doorbell so her roommates could retrieve her. As he quickly pulled away, he realized she had left her purse in his car, so in a final act of chivalry he made a U-turn and tossed her purse over his shoulder, landing it as close as he could to her doorstep as he drove on into the night.

The party was usually held at a place called The Old Mill, a castle-like structure with European décor and a big dance hall, where we had a live band. Of course there was drinking, and singing, and dancing, and a good degree of fooling around for some in the back rooms of whatever building we had rented for any particular year. Our reputation for partying at The Bowery followed us around some, so changing locations was necessary from time to time. Especially the year we had a topless girl as drummer in the band, which seemed to draw some attention, especially from the local police, who came uninvited and watched as everyone scattered into the parking lot while the topless drummer stopped playing the drums long enough to put on a shirt.

The Old Mill was our go-to location and we rented it under a different alias each year to avoid any legal issues that might come up. I remember Pi Kapp brother Tom Hurd tossing pumpkins, left over from a previous Halloween party, off the balcony at couples who were dancing on the floor below. He was a little drunk, and his aim was terrible, so we didn't bother him, and everyone dancing on the floor below seemed oblivious to his carrying on anyway. As I was leaving one year, I saw one unconscious brother, literally hanging from a coat rack on a wall with his coat still on and his arms dangling down to his waist. No one else seemed to notice him, and I don't know how he got down from the coat rack. As you can see, there was a lot going on at these parties.

For one of the annual university yearbook pictures, we gathered at the Old Mill and everyone dressed up in Roaring

Twenties outfits, which was the theme of The Bowery. C-Note and I stood in one of the window frames that dotted the second story of the building. If you look closely you can see me standing behind him, except he raised his hand to wave at the camera just as the photo was taken, thus blocking my one chance at notoriety. One unnamed brother stood near the front door, posing in a fashionable coat and hat, but sans any trousers, just his skivvies, in honor of the annual Bowery . . . which was never, by the way, held at 51 North Wolcott.

FORTY-ONE

Living on the Edge

At some point in the late Sixties, the tide turned. More and more people were against the war in Vietnam. Protests got bigger. Burning the American flag became one of the things protesters did. The government started to question us being there, and whether there was even a chance in hell we could win the war. Most of us already knew the answer. The government was just slow to realize it. Just before that happened, our sister unit in the US Army Reserves received orders to go to Vietnam. They were a transportation company like us, only their base was in Pleasant Grove, a town to the south of us. We found out they had been called to duty while we were at summer camp at a base in Yakima, Washington early in the summer. Some of Yakima's reservists had been called too, right out of their hometown. Soon, several Army guys with silver leaves on their uniforms showed up at our camp, unannounced, to inspect us. After we stood there at attention in lines, as these senior-looking soldiers walked in front of us and stared us down for a while, our commanding officer told us about our sister unit heading to Vietnam within the next few weeks. And the bad news was that our unit was next.

We were told that President Johnson was going to send 50,000 soldiers from the Reserves to Vietnam. The first half were leaving in June, and the next batch—our group, in other words—would be leaving in August. Our job would be to drive supply trucks along jungle paths while the Viet Cong shot at us from trees and dirt hideouts. Of course, some of us who had trained as advanced infantry scouts would be going on ahead, looking for the enemy hideouts and trying to stop them from shooting at our trucks or the person driving them. I figured I had about a .01% chance of coming back alive. Simple math.

It was a very long summer. Even though it was just a headline in a newspaper, I felt like I was living on the edge of the world, looking over a large precipice at my own imminent death. I wondered about all the men who had already given their lives to a lost cause. Some had gone willingly, some had been drafted, but all of them had died in an unwinnable war, as it turned out. My soldier buddies C-Note Anderson, Nellie (the coach of our Mudigas intramural team), Pat and I didn't talk about it much among ourselves. I think we were all depressed, and in this case talking didn't really help. I remember telling my girlfriend at the time about it, but there wasn't much she could say either. Nor could my parents. So I just waited, trying to fill up the time between June and August the best I could.

I worked for the Salt Lake City Water Department painting fire hydrants around the city, dated girls left over from having summer flings on California beaches, listened to the neighbors playing the latest rock hits through an open window across the street from my bedroom in the frat house, and dunked basketballs on the eight-foot hoop in the backyard. Only about a half dozen of us lived there in the summer, so it was eerily quiet most of the time; and without air conditioning in the house, there was nowhere to hide from the suffocating heat or the emotional weight of what would happen in August, when my buddies and I would pack up and leave for Vietnam.

The US Army had fought back hard that year against the Tet Offensive, a Viet Cong-led attack on South Vietnamese towns and US military posts, starting in January of 1968. It surprised our leaders, all the way to the White House where President Johnson sat, probably thinking about his comment that "war took away the life of young men full of promise who didn't even know their enemy." That's when people started to realize that this was a different war, and not in a good way. We had underestimated the enemy. And so that long, hot summer came . . . and went. And Johnson never called the second wave of Reserves to Vietnam. In the end, I think only five or ten thousand reservists actually went to 'Nam. None of us knew what they were thinking in Washington, but the idea of us going over there just sort of evaporated.

During that summer, perhaps for the first time, I began to think about what I might do if I didn't die in Vietnam. In an offhanded sort of way, it motivated me. I knew I couldn't stay in college forever. Maybe I could find a good life on the other side of college, where there might also be a little uncertainty; and even though it would probably mean less time hanging with my buddies, it might be worth it.

FORTY-TWO

Sex, Drugs, and Rock 'n Roll

K A KA THE stray cat got stoned while residing at 51 North Wolcott. It wasn't her idea. One of our Pi Kapp brothers, who was a little high on marijuana at the time, decided to exhale into a paper bag after taking a hit on a joint, and then inserted Ka Ka into the bag to see what would happen. After about a minute, he placed Ka Ka on the arm of a couch. Word spread quickly through the house about Ka Ka's condition, so we all started gathering in the living room near the arm of the couch, where Ka Ka quietly sat like a majestic lion in a daze for an hour or two without moving, staring ahead at nothing in particular. My frat buddy Lew had given her that name, but he didn't smoke pot. Neither had Ka Ka, up to that point.

Smoking marijuana wasn't mainstream in the frat house, but some of the brothers did it. One thing I noticed about them was that they were generally relaxed and easy-going, like Ka Ka, who was probably the first stoned cat in the history of the world. For kicks, some of our stoned brothers would hire a Pi Kapp driver to take them up to the top of the Avenue streets, where the car if handled properly could "catch air" now and then, as it came back down and crossed over the intersections. They said it was ten times better than any rollercoaster you could ride, especially if you were high. What was also interesting was how stoned brothers could sit around the house, or maybe on the front porch, and notice little details that you might normally miss in an unaltered state of mind, like the colors of flowers in the garden, or the colors of the flowers on your stylish floral shirt. "Wowwww," they might say. Or they might giggle, and get embarrassed if they thought they were chuckling too much. More than once, I heard a group of them sing the music lyric "Na Na Na Na, Na Na Na, Hey, Hey, Goodbye," to me as I left the house. To wrap up the day, some stoned brothers liked to listen to a local late-night radio talk show, where callers talked about all kinds of crazy things, like how their Winnebago had been acting up, and other "insipid" (to quote a brother) and fairly useless pieces of information you could probably never use in History 101. It was, in its own and different way, entertaining.

You might be surprised to hear this, but sex was also something for which brothers were discreet. It wasn't really a topic of discussion, pretty much kept behind closed doors, like smoking pot. If we talked about sex at all, it was in a light-hearted way, like the time one of our fraternity brothers was sharing his story of how he was resting in a sleeping bag, all zipped up with his girlfriend next to him, when her full-time military type dad made a surprise visit in her backyard. He didn't talk too long to her that night, which was a relief to the brother sharing the sleeping bag with her, and who needed to come up for air pretty soon. We speculated her father may have concluded she wasn't alone in the sleeping bag. Simple math.

I only knew of one brother, a handsome face-man

coincidentally, who got married before his time. It had been a hasty relationship, so to speak, and he had to leave school and change his life around so he could take care of his new wife and forthcoming baby. It was sad, really. I found out years later that everything worked out, but it wasn't in anyone's game plan at Pi Kappa Alpha to leave their beloved fraternity on short notice, even though accidents happen.

Live concerts were a major happening during this time, too. In 1969, the motorcycle gang, Hell's Angels, was hired to be "security" at a free Stones concert at the Altamont Speedway in California. When an 18-year-old man pulled a revolver near the front of the stage, one of the Angels stabbed him to death. There were at least two other deaths as well, from a car accident and a possible drug overdose. Mick Jagger sang their hit anthem that night, "Sympathy for the Devil," wearing a red cape. I have to admit I liked the Stones' musical ability, and the bluesy rhythms they created, and they were very good showmen—but I didn't like reading about someone dying at a rock concert. Not a good sign of things to come. The new psychedelic feel to rock concerts, the special lighting, and some of the music had an incendiary effect on the throngs of young people who came to concerts.

The pinnacle of rock concerts, of course, was Woodstock. It happened in Bethel, New York, 40 miles southwest of Woodstock, in August of 1969 on a big piece of dairy farmland owned by Max Yasgur. Max made $10,000 for the use of his land. Fifty thousand music lovers were supposed to attend. The promoters were surprised when they sold about 180,000 tickets, but over 400,000 people showed up and stuck around for the next three or four days, overrunning ticket booths, bathrooms and water stations. I didn't know anyone who went to Woodstock, but it became one of the biggest events in music history and is still called one of the defining moments for the

"Counterculture Generation." Creedence Clearwater Revival was the first group to perform and Jimi Hendrix was the last, playing for over two hours.

Music, especially rock 'n roll, probably defined the Sixties as much as anything. It somehow managed to push classical and jazz music aside starting in the late Fifties, and morphed by the mid-Sixties into something much more than just Elvis and Jerry Lee Lewis. It was an explosion of new sounds, and new ways of using instruments, usually by plugging them into electrical outlets. I loved music, and I followed the so-called music revolution in all its forms. The Beatles and the Rolling Stones probably did more to affect us musically than just about any other groups. But soon Jimi Hendrix, The Doors, Chicago, The Moody Blues, Santana, The Who, Crosby, Stills and Nash, Grand Funk Railroad, Steppenwolf, and a hundred other bands were creating music like we had never heard before. Live rock concerts became common, and top music groups were earning lots of money, which often led to extravagant and glamorous-looking lifestyles. There was a downside, too, as music groups often got lost in their new lives, fueling the idea that sex, drugs and rock 'n roll were freeing. The country was upside down with problems. Some were just looking for a way to put aside worries and concerns about the future. The music explosion, the sexual revolution, and any taking of new drugs, even if unproven, offered an escape from real life. Especially in college. But these were temporary fixes. The effects wore off. Ka Ka the cat was living proof.

FORTY-THREE

Life Eclectic

ONE REASON I became a member of Pi Kappa Alpha fraternity was to be around people I admired who didn't always think like me. I thought I could become a better person if I had lots of examples of what living a good life might look like. In a house of about a hundred men, diversity of thought and action could be inspiring, whether you shared the same values or not. Differing thoughts led to differing behavior. Brothers approached life the best they could. Some of our behavior got good results. Other behavior not so much. I learned from all of them, as well as from my own experiences during those very educational years. Come to think of it, my education hasn't ever really stopped. I think we all draw from the things going on in our lives, hopefully learning and growing and becoming better people each day.

I always liked the word "eclectic," which as an adjective means "deriving ideas, style or taste from a broad and diverse range of sources." I like to think our fraternity house was pretty eclectic. Diverse. No one way to reach a goal, get the job done. Like the brother from another fraternity who wore two different tennis shoes in an intramural touch football game. When asked why, he said his high-top shoe was good for cutting right or left, and his low-top shoe was good for sprinting. Personally, I think he just wore the wrong shoes that day, maybe lacing them up while still half asleep. Better than two left shoes, like my buddy Steve Bushnell wore for a pickup game of basketball. I wanted to find a good pair of shoes that might last me a long time, ones I could select from a variety of sources. I had to try on a few different pair before I found some that were comfortable.

During my search for a good fit in life, I discovered I was better at playing basketball than softball. I was better not skipping breakfast, and I enjoyed swimming more when I wore a swimming suit. I was better at attending classes during the midday than early or later in the afternoon. I had to study in spurts, not marathons. I read more books after college, becoming an avid reader in my later years, than I ever did when my job was pretty much to read full-time. When I became a manager in business, I told my staff to play to their strengths. Do the things you do well, continually improving rather than dwelling on or worrying about the things you don't do as adeptly. That strategy got us pretty good results in our business.

I also realized that I enjoyed looking at things from both sides. Some say this is overanalyzing, but no one ever accused me of that. I probably leaned to keep things on the surface, where I could avoid any conflict or give the appearance of being a deep thinker. You need to wear an argyle sweater and smoke a pipe if you want to do that. At least in college.

As a freshman, I signed up for a basketball class, which would fill a college requirement. Anything in PE, as they called it, would do. Unfortunately, a bunch of other people signed up for that class, too, and since my last name started with "S," I didn't make the cut. Instead, I was assigned to a beginning swimming class. Initially, I didn't think this was too bad. I liked swimming ever since my mother made me take a beginner's class one summer. I even became qualified to be a lifeguard by the time I was in high school. On the first day of class, though, the instructor told us we would all be swimming naked. I don't know if there was just a shortage of swimming suits or not, but I was dumbfounded. Really. Maybe I would have felt better if the class was co-ed, but probably not. Even wearing a Speedo would have been somewhat acceptable. Better than nothing, anyway. I swam in the class one time, in a big indoor pool at the university, staying in the water as much as possible, with all these other guys swimming laps back and forth in my vicinity. But that was it. I faked a sinus infection, and transferred to another PE class the next day. The university must have made some class adjustments for the next semester, because I never heard of anyone else who took a class where you swam naked. People have told me to get out of my comfort zone, but I don't think that is what they meant.

Another learning experience occurred one summer while I lived at the frat house, when a couple of brothers recruited me to play in a church softball game. They were short a few players, and they wanted me to fill in. Being a good brother, I agreed. Besides, I figured we'd probably stop to eat some burgers and fries on the way back to the frat house. I had usually played shortstop or second base when I was a little leaguer, but the team needed someone to play third base. During warmups, I thought I could impress the brothers by throwing a ground ball the coach hit to me to first base using my sidearm toss, which I could usually do with reasonable accuracy. So, I winged it to first with as much force as possible, making the speed pretty good but not my aim. It landed about three feet to the right of first base, right smack in the middle of the back of a player who was cleaning his cleats as he leaned against a fence. What complicated things was that he was on the other team. I think I caught him right in the middle of his back because the ball popped up in the air almost like it was coming off a bat. It sounded like it was coming off a bat, anyway. Time seemed to stop as he stood there facing the chain link fence with his hands on the top of the metal bar running across it. After shaking the fence for a few seconds, he slowly buckled, fell on his knees, and then laid on the ground face down. Even though it all seemed a little over dramatic to me, I became deeply concerned about his situation as he lay there on the ground. Did I really throw the ball that hard?

It was a long way from third base to the other side of first base. As I walked across the pitcher's mound to apologize to the guy sprawled out in the dirt and not showing any signs of life, I caught glimpses of my fraternity brothers. First there was JR "110%" Knight at shortstop, holding his glove in apparent embarrassment over his face, probably hoping no one would see him. Then on second base was Briant Herzog, only he was on his knees, and it looked like tears were coming out of his eyes and running down his face as he cradled his glove in his hands that hovered just over his lap. Our first baseman was nowhere to be seen. All this lack of support from my teammates made it an even longer walk to first base. My memory is vague about everything else that happened that night except a couple of things. One, the guy on the other team I hit with my errant throw was just fine, because he hit a line drive about 100 mph at me when he was at bat during the first inning. Two, we didn't stop for burgers and fries on the way home. And three, that was my last softball game with the church team. They evidently found someone else to play third base who probably didn't throw sidearm.

On an especially warm summer morning, one of the brothers showed up with a new bicycle, which he parked right in front of the front door at 51 North Wolcott. It had lots of gears and looked very sleek and speedy. He told me to take it for a spin.

Which I did. And it was indeed sleek and speedy, and went up hills really fast, especially if you went to a higher gear and peddled like crazy. The last thing I remember is getting close to the top of a pretty good hill, with the fairway of one of the holes on a golf course stretched out on the ride side of the road. The next thing I remember is being in the hospital, all bandaged up, with either catsup or blood staining the bandage wrapped around my head. Eric Ryberg and another fraternity brother just happened to be playing golf right there on that fairway, and came to my rescue. The doctor who was looking at me asked me if I had eaten breakfast before undertaking the hike up the hill, but I think he already knew the answer. He called it sugar deficit, something I hadn't really understood before that moment. I've eaten breakfast ever since, even if riding a bicycle isn't in my plan for the day.

College life, especially if it's coupled with fraternity life, gives you some time to figure things out. And all these eclectic experiences helped me make some decisions. About career, marriage, religion, philosophy, and all the little things that help make up the person I was becoming.

Most importantly, I learned that all the "eclectic" men of Pi Kappa Alpha were there for me, like frat brother Eric Ryberg who didn't finish his already-paid-for round of golf to take me to the hospital. Even though Bri Herzog (who became a doctor and tragically died of a stroke about a year ago) and JR Knight seemed to abandon me at the church softball game, I understood why they might not want to associate with me at that particular moment. They still gave me a ride home. Besides, I owed JR for not giving him the shirt off my back for his sprained ankle at a pickup basketball game. We called it good.

FORTY-FOUR

SMC

I PROBABLY WASN'T THE best candidate for house president (or "SMC" in the tradition of our particular fraternity) of the Alpha Tau chapter of Pi Kappa Alpha in 1970. I wasn't playing any sports for the university, I wasn't a student body officer, and my 2.7 GPA wasn't helping us be the number one fraternity academically, although most of my frat brothers helped us be at or near the top in sports and academics. If you hang around the house long enough, though, maybe guys think it's your time, looking at electing you as an endorsement to graduate and leave, perhaps.

I loved being SMC, though. Running chapter meetings, and being sort of the head cheese during Rush week, was fun for me. I think it's where I learned to develop better "people skills," which just means you can converse on a reasonably intelligent level with other people. It's not rocket science. Not even close. You didn't talk much about politics, or the war, girls, or even sports during Rush Week. What you talked about is what a great place Pi Kappa Alpha is as you conversed with potential future frat brothers. My brothers and I were typically on our best behavior. No one took a leak off the top of the house, or used profanity with the frequency it was normally used around the house. We all took showers and wore our best stuff. Hondo even hung up the blue bathrobe he wore some days while he studied for law school. Gordy Gee, future president of Ohio State University, often wore a bow tie and sports coat during Rush Week. We cleaned up pretty good, more or less.

My job was to say a few words as a welcome and introduction about the frat house during some of the events. Then we all circulated around, meeting rushees while we looked for active brothers who might have something in common with our guests.

I remember how wide-eyed I had been just a few years earlier, shaking the hands of upperclassmen who seemed so self-assured and confident. Granted, it was a different feeling now, being on the other side of those handshakes. But I knew I still had a lot to learn about living a good life to its fullest. I knew I had to pay some dues. I still sought out role models and people I admired, even from a distance, who could teach me more. Many of them were in or had graduated from the very fraternity I called my own for the past several years.

Every year, the Pi Kapps had a banquet to honor our fathers. As SMC, I was required to speak at the banquet. I looked up to my dad. He wasn't pretentious, caught up in himself, or prideful. He was an effective businessman, a devoted husband and father, and in his own way didn't let anyone take advantage of him or mistreat him. Once as a youngster, he took me to a five-and-dime store on a corner not too far from our house. He parked the car at the far end of a bus stop and took me shopping. On the way out, we noticed a bus parked behind our car, almost pinning it in. The bus driver had about a half a block behind him to park the bus, so it was obvious he was making a point. My dad apologized, but that wasn't enough for the bus driver. He started berating my father, maybe even pointing out that he wasn't a good example for his young son.

My dad thought that was enough, and he told the bus driver to back off, so to speak. A bit of a shouting match ensued, but it ended when my dad taught me a lesson. He told the bus driver he was out of line, way out of line. He'd apologized even though there was plenty of room behind the bus for, at the very least, another bus. Then he asked the bus driver for his name. The bus driver's demeanor changed instantly. He was hesitant. No longer abusive. I'm not sure if he ever gave my dad his name, but Dad looked at the front of the bus, made note of the route number, and told the bus driver he would be hearing from him. The driver quickly disappeared into the bus, and immediately pulled away.

That's not the only thing I learned from my dad, but it is one little ploy I've used from time to time when needed, which usually changes the complexion of a conversation, especially if you believe you have reason on your side.

At the banquet that night, I talked about my dad a little, who I came to appreciate more and more as I entered the world of business and started raising a family. I told the sixty or so fathers and sons packed into the living room of our fraternity house how being a Pi Kapp had molded and changed me, helped me grow up, and had taught me more than I had ever learned from all my university professors combined. I told the good men of Pi Kappa Alpha they stood as mentors, right behind my dad, who taught me how to work hard and take names if necessary.

1970

Tragedy at Kent State

Sometimes a new year—or in this case a new decade—can be a turning point. A time to change things up. Do things differently. Make a fresh start. That seemed to happen in 1970 almost subconsciously, as if the whole nation decided they'd had enough of the Sixties. Time to move on. Things got a little better. But not all the way better.

Charles Manson and his clan went on trial for their insidious Hollywood murders. Fourteen US Army officers were tried for the Mỹ Lai Massacre in Vietnam. The Army named its first two female generals, Anna Mae Hays and Elizabeth Hoisington. We actually had one day when no one died in Vietnam, and President Nixon withdrew 40,000 troops and offered a peace Treaty to Vietnam, but they rejected it. I think they knew they had us on the run.

Paul McCartney announced the end of the Beatles. The tobacco industry couldn't advertise on television anymore. The US launched Apollo 13 but an oxygen tank exploded in their space capsule, and the three astronauts had to return to Earth and abort their trip to the Moon. No one realized how close we came to losing them until Ron Howard made a movie about their harrowing ordeal years later. Ron Howard's days as Opie in *The Andy Griffith Show* were behind him.

In May, The National Guard opened fire on peaceful protestors at Kent State University in Ohio, killing four students. It was an event that shook everyone. We lost music legends Janis Joplin and Jimi Hendrix within three weeks of each other, possibly due to drug overdoses. They were both 27 years old. Gary Gabelich drove his Blue Flame rocket-powered speedster

622 mph on the Bonneville Salt Flats of Utah, establishing a world record that stood for 13 years. Garry Trudeau's comic strip *Doonesbury* debuted in 28 newspapers nationwide. It wasn't a bad year for people named Gary, as far as I can tell. Matt Damon, River Phoenix, Claudia Schiffer and Melissa McCarthy were born. Cartoonist and sculptor Rube Goldberg died, and so did Brian Piccolo, who played professional football for the Chicago Bears and was close friends with Gale Sayers. Their story of their friendship became a hit TV movie. But the Bears didn't win the Super Bowl. The Kansas City Chiefs did. Wisconsin Senator Gaylord Nelson organized the first "Earth Day" after a big oil spill off the coast of California. I don't know what he was doing in California. The top grossing movie was *Love Story*, with Ali McGraw and Ryan O'Neal. I couldn't bring myself to see it. The disaster movie *Airport* and the anti-war war movie *M*A*S*H* came in next, followed by *Patton*, starring George C. Scott as the rugged general of World War II. It won Best Picture. Maybe people took to it because we won that war.

American Motors introduced the Gremlin, making almost everyone wonder why anyone would christen a car with that name. Not to be outdone, Chevrolet introduced us to the Vega. NASA's spacecraft Explorer 1 burned up in the atmosphere after orbiting Earth for 12 years, thus missing the entire decade. Some of our citizens would probably have volunteered to go along for the ride, in retrospect. Others may have missed some of it anyway, especially if they were stoned. ABC Anchorman Chet Huntley retired. He'd probably had enough of the Sixties, too.

The best-selling album of that year was Simon and Garfunkel's *Bridge Over Troubled Water*. Indeed.

FORTY-FIVE

Mister Adventure

ERV TERRY, ONE of my very best friends going back to the 5th grade, who joined my fraternity after he finished jumping out of airplanes for the US Army Special Forces, was made for adventure. He humored me by joining my fraternity, and stuck around like a good brother, even though I suspect sitting on the front steps of the frat house didn't hold a candle for him to diving out of an airplane from a thousand feet above the ground. He was a wonderful athlete with a specimen body built for sports, but he loved hunting, fishing, hiking, and killing grizzly bears in Alaska more than making a twenty-foot jump shot on a basketball court. It was just the opposite for me.

Erv graduated in history from the university, so he must have done a lot better sitting through that TV history class I took. He loved history. I sometimes hear people say that history "repeats itself." But I didn't see that happen much when I was struggling through school, except for my propensity to earn a C+ in just about every class I took. Erv said there was a lot to learn from history, though. So soon after he graduated, he left with C-Note and Mitty for Alaska where they all started selling copiers for Xerox, which really didn't have much if anything to do with history. But evidently a bunch of ideas about making bank in Alaska were swimming around in their heads, as we got closer to closing the door on life on the front porch of 51 North Wolcott, and college too. We kept in touch with letters and get-togethers whenever they came down to the "Lower 48."

The guys kept telling me to join them in Alaska, or at least come up for a visit, but I had my hands full trying to wrap up my own college career and figure out what to do next. Alaska, as much as I loved my dear brothers, didn't fit into the mix. In a few years they would leave Xerox, buy some nice houses, get married, and start their own real estate development business. Not necessarily in that order. And they continued to make bank, over and over. Within another few years, they were buying more houses, and lodges, and airplanes and boats, and they spent time using these pretty wonderful toys to fish for salmon and halibut, and hunt deer, elk and, yes, even bears. Erv later told me he killed a grizzly while camping in the snowy wilderness a plane ride away from Anchorage, his new home town. The bear evidently wanted to try some of the fish Erv had been pulling out of the icy waters, and Erv wasn't sharing. But he had a rifle that was perfect for shooting grizzly bears and other big things up there in Alaska, so he used it on this huge specimen of an animal, watching it drop dead about ten yards from him. You can see why I didn't think it was such a good idea to go to Alaska. I had survived riding with Erv in his MG sports car in high school, but landing a single-engine Cessna 185 with him on the cold water in Alaska, and confronting grizzly bears armed only with a rifle, was a whole different deal.

Erv married Linda Muhlestein, a wonderful girl from our high school, who followed him up to Alaska. She was adventurous too, so they got married and started a family. Walt and Andy also got married. I think Walt married his high school sweetheart while Andy met a terrific looking girl in Alaska. About a dozen collective children later, all three were still making bank, so they started an air freight business in Alaska, once again eclipsing the economic curve right there in the snow, where more and more people were venturing even though it was dark more than half the time. They were really smart guys, as you can tell. And by now multi-talented in business as well as hunting, fishing and flying their single-engine planes all over what is known as "the bush" in Alaska. Linda once told me it feels like paradise up there. Just colder.

At some point, they started relaxing a little more since all their businesses were, more or less, just rolling along. They bought some houses in southern Utah and Arizona, and nourished the lodge they owned in Alaska. Erv started dabbling in the air freight business in other parts of the world, including Cambodia and the rest of Southeast Asia, where I believe he was buying and selling airplane parts, dealing with the heads of all these other governments. He developed quite a list of who's-who clients when it came to foreign leaders. He once told a mutual friend, Clark Alvey, that one of the governments he had a good relationship with wanted him to place an unbelievable amount of money in an investment for them, and take a hefty commission for doing it. Erv did his homework on things like this, so he walked away when he found out it was marked money.

It was in Cambodia where he almost died, lying on the side of the road in a jungle. He had crashed his motorcycle in a somewhat deserted area. He might not have made it back to see his wife and three sons except that a man from Chicago stopped to save his life when none of the natives seemed to notice him. Erv was Mister Adventure. Being a little shy, he didn't talk a lot about things. I think it was either U-Haul or C-Note who told me about Erv's crash in the jungle. Even after that, he still had a hard time staying put for too long, which is something I noticed early on, when he started disappearing from the front steps of 51 North Wolcott.

FORTY-SIX

Finals

SOONER OR LATER, I knew I had to graduate. Start doing all the things I said I would when I began my college career and took the infamous History 101 course on TV. It was inevitable. I started checking off the boxes next to the classes I needed to finish up before leaving, and the list got smaller and smaller. Every year. I was on a collision course with graduation; and for the life of me, I couldn't see a way out.

I had actually taken enough undergraduate courses that I could almost graduate with a couple of different degrees, one of them in English, my favorite subject. Some of my friends were going on to graduate school, which was a good way of putting off the reality that you would eventually have to take up residency in the real world. By then you would probably be set for life. My C+ GPA wouldn't allow me a chance in heaven like that. Even if it did, school would be much more serious, with no one really sitting next to me except highly intelligent people who probably all got A+ grades as undergrads. There wouldn't be any sneaks or parties with cute girls or any guys sleeping on roofs, either. It wouldn't be a good fit for me.

I couldn't figure out what to do with an English degree

except teach, which I had been on the other side of somewhat unsuccessfully. As a business major, I had to take Statistical Analysis, a three-part series, and pass each course with at least a C- in order to graduate. I think they called the classes Accounting 129, 139, and 149. They were all in a foreign language to me and included all kinds of math equations and plus/minus kinds of tests I absolutely knew I would never use in a lifetime. I put off taking these classes as long as possible, almost to the very end.

Most classes were structured so that you took a couple of midterms and a final exam. It didn't seem to matter how hard I studied—when the professor passed out their little "blue book" full of lined paper on which you wrote the answers to the questions they wrote on the board, my mind would often just go blank. Where was my brilliant sister when I needed her? One of my friends, when seeing the questions on the board for a different class he needed, felt overwhelmed and decided to take a brief nap. When he told me the story, he said he'd been up most of the night studying. While he slept with his head down on his desk, the guy next to him, a supposed friend, stuck bubble gum in his blue book so that he couldn't even open it for the test. Imagine having to explain away the bubble gum to a professor at the end of the exam. I mean, there was no way out. No way at all.

When I looked at some of the questions for these tests, I wondered if maybe I'd forgotten to buy one of the books for the class. Somehow, I got through 129 and 139 with at least a C- and without any bubble gum stuck inside my blue book. Now 149 was looming, the last class I had to take before I could graduate. C- was all I needed. I got a D. What made matters worse was that it was spring semester, and in a few weeks I was supposed to be seated in the university football stadium, capped and gowned, to receive my graduation diploma in front of my parents and a few girls I hoped might notice too. In anticipation, I had prepaid for my cap and gown and was headed over to the bookstore to pick them up, except I made a stop at the professor's door who taught Accounting 149. Others were crowded around the door, looking for their names listed on a long yellow sheet of lined paper stuck to the thick, glass-paned window hiding the professor on the other side. Most of them were saying things like "all right," "yes," and even "what a relief." None of those expressions fit me at the moment, as I stood there looking at the extra bold letter "D" next to my name.

I didn't pick up my cap and gown. I didn't walk down the graduation aisle in front of my parents and others with my C+ diploma. Instead, I took the class again, that summer when it wasn't as hot as it was at Camp Roberts or Fort Irwin in Death Valley . . . but it was close. The class was held on Monday and Wednesday evenings from 7 to 10 pm. Once again, I could imagine hundreds of cute girls running around campus or in the streets all over the city while I sweated away, trying for a C- or maybe even a C+ just one more time. The words "ironic" and "déjà vu" floated around in my head a lot that summer. But I stayed the course. Literally. And happily, I ended up with a C+, which felt more like an A+ at that particular moment. Now I could legitimately say "all right," or even scream "yeaahhh" in all honesty. Unfortunately, I don't remember anyone else standing there when I saw my name on the door that hid the professor on the other side. But I didn't need him anymore. I was done! Or at least that's what I thought.

FORTY-SEVEN

A letter from Pat

MY FRIENDSHIP CONTINUED to blossom with Pat Roylance, my pledge brother and Army buddy, during the time we wrote letters back and forth after he graduated, got married, and went to work for Congressman Gunn McKay in Washington, D.C. We corresponded almost weekly. I hoped I sounded as intelligent and insightful as he did. And funny. His letters were usually quite funny. Except one.

It arrived about the time I was graduating. I thought it would be just like any other letter, full of humor, wisdom, and funny things that had happened since our last dialogue. But it wasn't. Pat told me he hadn't been feeling well. No energy. Hard to get things done. He had to cut back on his morning exercise plan, and especially jogging around his neighborhood. His feet were sore, and he started showing some bruising on his heels. He went to the doctor, and after a battery of testing they diagnosed him. He had leukemia.

I didn't know much if anything about leukemia, but I could tell from his letter that it wasn't good. He might have even hinted that it could lead to his dying some years down the road.

I put away the letter. I knew I had to write back to him. Soon. But I was so sad, and not ready to respond. It was the first time someone I really loved and admired had gotten sick or even might've died.

By now he had started a family, was active again in his church, and was loving life in Washington D.C., with everything in the world to look forward to. I believe he had a beautiful daughter around one or two years old, and another baby coming soon. His wife Matty and he were probably more in love than ever. I just couldn't understand it. I couldn't reconcile it. I still don't understand things like this. There are no easy answers.

I did write to him. Offered my support and said that I thought he might get better. We kept writing back and forth. He didn't talk much about it but said enough for me to know that the disease was progressing. One of the options was a bone marrow transplant, something that was very cutting-edge, and very difficult to get because it was so new. And not highly successful. But there was a chance.

Over time, the bone marrow transplant began to look like the only way out for him. It took a while, but he received approval to have one. He had to fly to Los Angeles to get it, and he came through Salt Lake on the way there, bringing Marilyn and two beautiful little girls with him. His mother, who lived in a condominium on a canyon road just above the valley of the city, hosted a party for him. Pat and I had some time alone, and stood out on the balcony overlooking the bright city lights below.

He said two things I'll always remember. After some brief joking around, he got contemplative: "Mike, everyone dies. It just happens. The only difference between me and you is that I just happen to have a pretty good idea of when I will die. We're not that different." He said that, I think, to normalize what he was going through. Then he said, "But I'm thinking that maybe, just maybe, I might be a pathway for you to develop some faith in God." It seemed ironic that here he was, embracing God knowing he might die, while I was thinking he should be mad at God, like I was at the moment. I can't remember what I said in response, but it wasn't so eloquent. I think I might have had a few tears in my eyes. Maybe he did, too. I wished we would have hugged then. I wish I would have committed to him to do the very thing that over time I did anyway, mostly because of him. He made such a difference in my life, but that was our last conversation. He went to Los Angeles where he caught pneumonia, a common side effect of his disease, and passed away before they could do the bone marrow transplant.

I was numb at the funeral. Emotionless, sort of. I knew I had to be, because I didn't want to start wailing away in the back of the congregation. I may have been a pallbearer, but I'm not sure. Everything blurred together that day. Marilyn spoke at the funeral. Eloquently. I stayed in touch with her for a while. We had lunch a few times when she came to town. But I lost track of her, like others who meant so much to me.

The other letter I remember most from Pat was the one he wrote to me right after we met, when I had doubts about which fraternity to join. He was joining Pi Kappa Alpha, and he told me he thought it would be a good place for both of us to spend a few years together. Boy, were those good years. Every one of them.

FORTY-EIGHT

Graduating with Honors

IT TURNS OUT I did use Accounting 129, 139 and 149 after I graduated. Luckily, I found others who could do the math, but all the testing and statistical analysis I learned about in class came in handy during my career in marketing, as my associates and I tried to dissect what various segments of the population were thinking and doing. That was so we could prepare advertising messages to help them understand that the very best thing they could do was buy our client's products, and maybe live happily ever after. I didn't know this, however, on the day I found my C+ grade on the door of the professor who taught Accounting 149, the last class I would ever need to take at the university.

All buoyed up with the thought of my imminent graduation, I went straight to the Registrar's office to pick up my diploma. I had wasted some money on the cap and gown, but I wasn't upset about that anymore. The woman behind the window asked for some identification and then went looking for my diploma. Several minutes passed. It shouldn't be taking this long, I thought. Eventually she returned empty-handed. "I don't have a diploma for anyone with your name," she said matter-of-factly. "In fact, I don't have any record of you ever attending the university."

"But you've seen me at your window before, when I've checked out of classes," I pleaded.

"Yes, I've seen you before, for sure," she replied. Again, pretty matter-of-factly. Then she paused contemplatively and said these words that still sit pretty prominently in my head: "Maybe you graduated last semester."

I told her, "No, that isn't possible, because I flunked a class more or less that I needed to graduate."

She disappeared and then reappeared quickly, holding a nice, fake red leather case which she presented to me as I looked at her dumbfounded, probably in about the same way I looked at my professors in Accounting 129, 139 and 149. "They graduated you anyway," she informed me. She seemed to look at me like she was thinking *maybe they had enough of you.*

So, that's how I finished my college career. With the nice lady at the Registrar's office smiling, both of us realizing I hadn't really needed to take Accounting 149 again that summer, every Monday and Wednesday from 7 to 10 pm for a couple of months in the heat of the night.

I keep the diploma in the red case on the credenza in my home office these days. Yes, it's ironic that I really didn't need another C+ to graduate. I already had enough of them. But in an offhanded way, it capsulizes my life at the university. Puts a ribbon around it. Sometimes I wonder, though, if the ultimate irony might be the university calling me up someday and saying, "We're sorry to inform you that you really didn't graduate. You flunked that Accounting 149 class you needed, so we want your diploma back." It doesn't haunt me, because I figure I've made it this far in life, and I think I'll be okay whether or not the university puts their stamp of approval on my college career. And even with a C+ report card throughout,

I did learn things in and out of the classroom that have carried me along, and that I've been able to apply successfully to my post-college career and life in general. It's very clear that I wouldn't be the person I am today without a college education. I recommend college. And fraternity or sorority life, too. I think they complement each other quite nicely.

Here's just one more irony: Not once. Not ever. Not even one single time has anyone ever asked me how I did in my college classes. No one has ever asked for my GPA. My wife never has. My kids haven't. And no one I ever interviewed with for a job asked for my transcripts. If they had, I think I would have just shown them the fake red leather binder with my diploma in it, and told them I figured some things out while I was in college, even though all I had to show for it was a C+ here and there.

FORTY-NINE

Love and Friendship

ONE OF THE things I realized during my frat and college days was how important it is to have good friends. And to be good at communicating with others. Communication. It's the essence of a good relationship. They have a whole degree in communications at the university, but I'm not sure they teach how to be a really good communicator. You have to learn that on your own. Studying helps, but it comes down to something else: trial and error.

For a long time, I thought I was good at communicating. But I wasn't. Especially with girls I was dating. I always wanted to look good, so dating was more about "show and tell" than really communicating, or learning something important about someone else. Sometime after dating a hundred girls that didn't work out, I had an epiphany: they weren't the problem. I was. I was about leaving if things didn't go well. I was about "winning the game," so to speak. It didn't have anything to do with winning, though.

I looked back on past relationships and I realized I kept them pretty much on the surface. I thought acting cool and aloof would win the day. I thought saying funny things and being entertaining would keep their interest. I thought I could fill up the night with fun activities. Not that any of that was bad. But what I failed to realize was that it takes more. You might feel like you were in love with someone, but were you friends? Did physical attraction come with a meeting of the minds, too? In my experience, there was plenty of physical attraction out there but not necessarily good communication. That's where a communications degree from the university that taught people how to communicate would come in handy.

I figured out over time, reading up on the subject as much as I could from books that weren't required in class, that it takes a willingness to open up to someone as you learn what makes them who they are. Witty dialogue isn't enough. It might lead to a connection, but it doesn't always lead to a trusting relationship. You have to be yourself. Which gives the other person a chance to be themselves, too.

This thought process began when I was on a deep-sea fishing trip with Steve Bushnell, my Pi Kapp brother who had by now amassed a pretty good fortune selling swimming pool covers to movie stars in California. He purchased a 35-foot boat with his Pi Kapp business partner, Lanny Smith, and we headed to the Gulf of California, where we launched their new boat at San Filipe. A friend of theirs rounded out our rather inexperienced crew. The trip lasted over a week, until the Mexican Coast Guard turned our boat around in the bay of Bahía *de los Ángeles*, since we didn't have a boat permit, and sent us home. We tried to tell them the guy who issues boat permits in San Filipe decided to go binge drinking with some buddies, and had already been gone for a few days when we got there. People around town said it could be a week before he returned. Even though that was the truth, the Coast Guard— with their relatively huge speed boat with large guns welded to it—began eyeing our boat, perhaps for some parts they could use or sell. We made the prudent decision to leave, sensing that our situation could change rather quickly.

On the way down we caught a lobster big enough to feed the four of us for days. We snorkeled in clear blue waters and drifted along tall canyon-like cliffs, with expensive looking houses that appeared to be miniatures way up on the rocky cliffs above. But we never saw another person until the bay at Bahía *de los Ángeles*. Hundreds of miles away from anyone, I began to evaluate all my past relationships, good and bad. And there were plenty of good ones. Why hadn't they become more serious? Part of that was timing. Great girls and I crossed paths but met up at the wrong time for one or the other of us. I also concluded that you can't have a terrific relationship with someone if you don't take a risk sooner or later.

So, I changed how I approached dating, and relationships in general. The end game wasn't going to be one where I was victorious, necessarily, and completely won her over. Or where I would feel defeated and rejected. I decided the end game would be whatever it ended up being, with no expectations of how it would turn out. If someone said, "You're not my type," which happened with some degree of frequency, I was okay with that. If I wasn't right for them, then why try to make it a game I could win? If they were ready to move on, even after one date, then I was too. I wasn't interested in spending a lifetime trying to prove something to someone else. Sure, you see a lot of rom-com-type movies where the relationship is all over the place, until at the very end when the girl or the guy realizes, "What was I thinking? You're perfect for me." Of course, the audience knows this all along, which is something you would think the characters would figure out too. Early. Within about 30 minutes of the movie starting.

The great thing was, I was no longer playing a part in a movie. It was no longer a contest. It was no longer a battle. Along the way, I began to see the importance of being in the moment, of keeping agreements, of valuing others, and especially valuing myself. What this all did was give me a degree of power I hadn't felt before. I also wanted to empower the girl on the other side of the table so she could be herself. Or not. Some girls were still hiding out, not risking letting themselves out of the bag, like I had done before.

It was during this time that I had the most fun getting to know girls I was dating. My hope was to be more authentic. More genuine. And just let things unfold naturally. No date was a bust. Not anymore. I decided to have fun on every date no matter the outcome. And, I would make it as much fun as I could for the other person. I can't say I was completely successful. I can't say I was entirely forthright or candid every moment. But there was hope for me. I was on a better path. And with practice, it was easier to drop the pretenses and be who I was trying to be: a good person, but not perfect, and not putting on the smooth armor of coolness that I had tried to wear unsuccessfully for years. That wasn't who I was, I discovered.

FIFTY

A Most Unusual Cast of Characters, Reprise

IT NEVER DAWNED on me that the fraternity house on 51 North Wolcott might be likened to a big circus tent, with all kinds of crazy things going on inside, until I started reminiscing while sketching out some notes for this book. Something was always happening there. Day and night. Except for the hours between 4 am and 10 am, approximately, when the house needed time to recover from the previous day's events. Otherwise, activity around the house was nonstop. Someone always had a story to tell, or somewhere to go, dragging curious brothers along. Or things just started unfolding inside, undetected by everyone except the watchful neighbors, like getting Ka Ka the cat stoned, dumping a ton of sand in the front room for a party, opening a keg for a sorority exchange on a Friday afternoon, or shooting dart guns at each other with only a makeshift flag at stake, or engineering the greatest sneak in frat history with a U-Haul van, or even attempting to start a marijuana farm under someone's bed. Or having some young lady dance around the living room partially unclothed. Almost like in a circus.

Despite all this pandemonium, The Pi Kapps I knew during my residency grew disproportionately for the good, and figured things out in ways that made their lives better. Made the world around them better, too. With few exceptions, they ended up in very good places.

Today U-Haul Johnson lives in the hot desert of St. George, Utah, recently called the fastest growing city in the US. He has a stylish little cottage he shares with his wonderful wife, Alaris, just off the 12th hole of a prestigious golf course, where he plays almost every day, despite having had close to 30—that's right, 30—shoulder, back and neck surgeries, all due to a degenerative arthritis condition he has had for years. He never talks about it or complains. Once he showed me a huge jar with metal screws, balls, sockets, and other hardware that came right out of his body whenever he needed more surgery. We stay in touch when he comes this way for surgery or other things. He still dabbles as a consultant in his profession, helping people rehabilitate mentally after having traumatic things happen to them. You might say it's right up his alley. One day, he said he didn't think he'd accomplished all that much in his life in retrospect. And I said, "Rex, you're 'U-Haul Johnson,' the guy who engineered the greatest sneak in the history of fraternities. You are famous, or at least you should be." I'd like to make him famous, too. I really would. Andy Warhol, the world-renowned visual artist during the '60s who painted all kinds of things, including some Campbell's Soup cans, supposedly said, "In the future everyone will be world famous for 15 minutes." I would like to officially nominate Rex for his moment in the sun. He's overdue.

Scott "Hondo" Welling lives in Midway, Utah, which might be the second fastest growing city in the USA. He bought a farmhouse there, where the snow can pile up and almost cover his front door during some of the colder winters. He commutes to Park City and practices law with Brent Gold, the Pi Kapp brother who tried to masquerade as Bill Russell in our Lakers vs. Celtics game at a local gym back in 1968. Brent lives with his wife in Park City, and until recently played county recreational basketball at the local gym up there. Lou Hudson, the former basketball star of the Atlanta Hawks, lived there too. They played against each other once in a while, but I don't think Brent ever tried to wear a Bill Russell-type goatee in the games.

Glenn Holley, my little brother in the fraternity, builds houses and loves camping and hiking all over Utah. He's the frat brother who told Tamie, my wife-to-be, that she deserved a medal when he first met her over dinner in Park City one night. He said it to her right out loud in front of us, in a somber, almost regretful tone. I was hoping for something more along the lines of "you're marrying the greatest guy in the world," just in case she had any doubts. Glenn and I rented a house for a while during our post-college years, dating girls and listening to Pink Floyd over our sound system that could shake the house down to the foundation. That's when we burned some baby back ribs in a Crockpot, something people were astounded we could even do. They said it was unheard of. But Glenn had other skills. He built a desk for me that sits in my home office today. It's made out of a wooden door with 4x4 legs as anchors. I put a piece of glass over the top. When my wife hired an interior decorator to spruce up our place, she walked through the house and looked in my study. "That stays!" she said, pointing to the desk. "That is something Frank Lloyd Wright would have made." I paid $125 for it.

J.R. Knight and I play some golf, and he helps me invest in things that usually make money. I owe him a lot. He told me he'd like to shed the nickname "110%," because he doesn't think it reflects who he is. But I disagree. He coaches soccer and basketball teams all over the place, and his kids have learned what it means to commit to giving everything you have out there on the playing field or the basketball court. Or anywhere else, for that matter. It's true that he is a lot more than his nickname, but it's a good name. Better than "90% Knight," for sure.

"Nordy" is retiring from his career of teaching and being some kind of CIA operative. He doesn't live close by, but he keeps in touch with Hondo and some of the others. Whenever we get together, we make him throw his imaginary backwards baseball pitch he developed while he was playing for the university. He's still the life of the party. Hard not to love "Nordy." Or the big grin he can flash at you through those jowls and dimples at the start of his make-believe pitcher's throw.

"The Heat" is still an enigma. Hondo told me he lives in Alaska and has a fishing guide and touring business. And kids, and the wife he married sometime after he left 51 North Wolcott. He and "WOAPL" (Craig Boorman, aka "Worst Of All Possible Links"), played softball up there when it wasn't too dark, and they were a menacing duo on any team, especially when Jon was throwing the ball anywhere in the playing field. Both great athletes. Legendary type guys. I think WOAPL is stateside again, but I've lost track of him, too.

I saw "C-Note" Anderson and Walter "Mitty" Hanni when they were in town a couple of years ago. We had dinner in St. George with Rex and our wives. We all looked older. They spend more time in warm places since they really didn't need to be somewhere cold all the time. I doubt Andy is limber enough to jump out the window of the frat house to avoid getting sneaked by the pledges anymore. I know I'm not.

Al "Bwana" Bluth has his own physical fitness enterprise.

Our paths cross now and then. He lives in Heber, Utah, which might be the third fastest growing city in America. He and his high school sweetheart, Mary, have great kids who are taking over for him, so he can do what he wants and "hang ten" more with Mary. He still has some Hawaiian shirts and gets over to his old stomping grounds now and then.

As of this writing, Scott Anderson is still the president of one of the most successful banks anywhere around. I think they told him some years ago he had to retire at a certain age, but since things were moving along so well, they changed their minds. Scott does lots of charity work, too—but neither of us have served dinner to anyone important, like we did for the active men of Pi Kappa Alpha when we were pledges and they all got sick. The word got around that we can't be trusted, evidently.

Gordy Gee, Nolan Bushnell and Karl Rove have gone on to gain national fame and attention. They had that in them all the time, but I like to think Pi Kappa Alpha didn't hurt them, either. Maybe gave them a little bit of a boost, like the second stage of a rocket launched to the Moon or some other destination in space.

Charlie "Bus" Seldin, Bob Bernick and Rod Decker have retired from their writing gigs, but still dabble in their professions. Charlie does a lot of pro bono work now, and plays a little golf now and then. Bernick and Decker were investigative reporters for local news media, and you didn't want them on your tail if you were on the other side of doing the right things.

Craig Zwick, Don Pugh and Gary Sandberg have also retired, pretty much. They ran highly successful family businesses in which they probably still dabble, and now spend some time serving in their church and the community philanthropically. Don's body, as far as I know, completely healed after we took him to the hospital with a broken leg in the fourth game of our version of the 1968 Lakers-Celtics championship series.

Nellie worked for the government doing tax and accounting kinds of things before he retired. I see him whenever we have a high school reunion lunch or any kind of fraternity get together. I think he retired the trench coat he wore to coach the "Mudigas" intramural team. One of the funniest guys you could ever know, except when he has his game face on, which he wore all the way to the intramural flag football championships back in the day.

I love Lew Bautista, too. Even though he abandoned me to make a fortune in probably the second coldest place in America, Minneapolis, Minnesota. We still laugh about the good old days together, listening to Miles Davis, looking for girls in the streets at night, playing tennis in the hot summer days until we almost dropped. And eating pizza and jogging together late into the evenings. You wouldn't think those two activities went together, but we found a great pizza place about five miles from home, which we would use as a reward for running there. Running back was a lot more challenging. Today he lives in Lakeside, Arizona. It's cool there, in the mountains where he built a large log cabin home with lots of land and trees all around. He and his wife take in their grandkids whenever they show up, which is constantly.

Steve Bushnell and I hit it off playing hoops in high school and stayed friends, even after he wore two left shoes to a pickup basketball game with me. He married a beautiful young woman who was thirteen years his junior. Her parents were probably as reticent as Tamie's mom when we were getting engaged. Steve and Paula live in Oceanside, California, and Steve nurtures 250 acres of garden soil in Peru for flowers he grows and sells on the open markets throughout the US. He's the one who told me I'd never get married, and after I proved him wrong by asking Tamie to marry me, both he and his business partner, Lanny, coincidentally got engaged to their own girlfriends. Lanny, even called me from Washington, D.C. right after he proposed to say, "Thank you! I figured if you could do it, anyone could." I took it as a vote of confidence.

FIFTY-ONE

Real Life

ERV TERRY AND I stayed close over the years. He chided me for not coming to Alaska, which is what I should have done. But we called each other and talked. Or stayed in touch through emails. And grabbed lunch or shot hoops or just got together whenever he came home. But he never told me anything about losing his father in a swimming accident when Erv was just five years old. His father had a heart attack while the family was swimming in a lake not far from their home. He was helping Erv learn how to swim when it happened. Before he died, he managed to get Erv to the shore. His brother and sisters were there that day too, I think, and I can't imagine the effect on their family, and maybe on Erv more than anyone. He probably blamed himself and carried the weight of that moment throughout his life. Enough of a weight that he rarely shared it. He kept it hidden under that easy-going persona. I think he might have been thinking about that during Ingress at Pi Kappa Alpha, which is when I saw him act uncharacteristically, like someone in prison, fighting to break out. Maybe that's why he was always a little elusive, and though a wonderful friend you could always count on, prone to taking treks alone into the wilderness, whether it was in the nearby mountains of Utah or the bush country of Alaska or the jungles of Cambodia. Yet I think Erv was happy. He made the most of every day, raised a family, found a lot of success in business, and killed a grizzly bear on the side.

Once he told me he had a kidney removed. "Why?" I asked.

"Oh, it just wasn't working properly," he answered. "Had to get rid of it."

I knew there was more to the story. Years later, I heard from Linda or "Andy" or U-Haul Johnson that he had had a bout with cancer. It came again later, and he just endured. During the last few years of his life, Erv denied having it. He would tell me all was fine. Linda would say, "No, he's not fine. He's been given six months to live." In front of Erv she would proclaim his mortality. I changed the subject whenever this conversation emerged, but I knew she was just trying to prepare me, and maybe herself too, for what was coming.

Rex, Erv and I had dinner one night when he was in town in 2017. We dined at a little restaurant in Sugar House, a thriving neighborhood on the edge Salt Lake City. We had a great visit. Some good laughs. I took him back to the home Linda grew up in, where they were staying for a while. I saw him a couple more times before he passed away. My wife Tamie and I had dinner at his home in St. George with Linda. She cooked up a fabulous meal and we visited. When Erv and I were alone, I told him I loved him. He said he loved me too, something neither of us had ever said to each other before. We hugged and Tamie and I left. He died soon after, early one morning while taking a shower.

Rex spoke at his funeral. He had Andy and me stand next to him for moral support. I felt awkward standing up there next to Rex, but he delivered an eloquent tribute to Erv Terry, Mr. Adventure. At the family gathering after, I talked about our camping trip to the secret lake with hundreds of cutthroat trout we never caught. It's a funny story, but I mostly cried as I recalled it.

Erv Terry was an adventurer like you read about in books or watch in movies, like the Indiana Jones trilogy. He was also as physically fit as anyone I've ever known. He was the last one of us I thought could ever die. Real life wasn't everything I thought it would be. But Erv gave me a great reminder of what real life really is. On that night in St. George, after dinner he leaned over to me and said, "This has been a great life, okay?" (Erv often finished a sentence with "okay," making it sound like a question even though it was a statement.)

"With more to come," I said, looking at him head-on. But he didn't answer me. He just smiled and brushed his hair back with his strong, muscular hand.

---------------------- 1971 ----------------------

When will it be 1972?

1971 was both a good year and a bad year for me. Good because I graduated from college. Bad because I graduated from college. I can't speak for others, but good and bad things happened in 1971, like most other years. Unlike the mid to late Sixties, though, this year stacks up as pretty innocuous. There were definitely some highlights, and they were impressive. For starters, two more NASA expeditions, Apollo 14 and 15, made it all the way to the Moon. Both landed safely and returned home again. During the second mission, Astronauts David Scott and James Irwin became the first men to ride around on the Moon's surface in a dune buggy. It almost seemed like science fiction.

The landmark television series *All in the Family*, with Carroll O'Conner as the politically incorrect head of the household, began its eight-year run on national TV. It wouldn't fly today. A 6.6 earthquake hit Los Angeles. Satchel Paige became the first African American named to the Baseball Hall of Fame. The US, USSR and the UK signed a treaty banning the use of nuclear weapons on the ocean floor. *How about the rest of the planet,* some of us were asking?

The war in Vietnam was still raging, but the *New York Times* began to publish the Pentagon Papers, which revealed things the government was not telling us. A throng of anti-war protestors marched on Washington, trying to disrupt the government's workday. Twelve thousand demonstrators were arrested.

Both Charles Manson and Lt. William Calley Jr. received the death penalty. Calley led the raid in South Vietnam, referred to as the Mỹ Lai Massacre, that killed almost 500 unarmed civilians. He served three years of house arrest after his conviction. Manson remained a threat to society until his death in prison. Whenever you saw a photo of him, the guy who convinced several others to go with him to kill actress Sharon Tate, he had a crazed look in his eyes. It was eerie.

Future Olympian skier Picabo Street was born. Mark Wahlberg, who did a modeling stint in his underwear before becoming an actor, was also born, but I don't think they ever dated. Igor Stravinsky, famous composer, died. Trumpeter and throaty singer Louis Armstrong also passed away, and Jim Morrison, lead singer for the Doors, died in a bathtub in Paris at age 27.

The South Tower of the World Trade Center in New York City was completed, making it the second tallest building in the world at 1,362 feet. Disney World opened in Florida. A national poll indicated that 60% of the US population was against the Vietnam War, and President Nixon began bringing troops home. By mid-summer, there were less than 200,000 troops there, the fewest since 1966.

The Pittsburgh Pirates beat the Baltimore Orioles to win the World Series, but the Baltimore Colts beat the Dallas Cowboys in Super Bowl V, so Baltimore had something to celebrate after all. And the Milwaukee Bucks won the NBA Championship, the first expansion team to do so, somehow ending up with a couple of pretty good players: Lew Alcindor (who would change his name later that year to Kareem Abdul-Jabbar) and Oscar Robertson. Who would have thought? Or who would have thought Joe Frazier would defeat Muhammad Ali? But he did, at Madison Square Garden in New York City.

There were riots at Attica Prison in New York, and the National Guard had to intervene, resulting in the deaths of 32 inmates and 11 hostages.

Maybe the best thing about it 1971 was that 1972 was up next. The stock market would make a run too, signaling better times ahead. And the war in Vietnam was winding down. We all hoped so.

FIFTY-TWO

Things Keep Changing

WHEN I WAS preparing to graduate, I registered with the University Placement Center. They arranged interviews for graduating seniors with various well-known national and local businesses. My first interview was supposed to be with Macy's, the famous department store with a big reputation. I sat nervously in a waiting room while I filled out a very long questionnaire. And, I waited. And watched others come and go from the same interview.

I decided one thing: this wasn't for me. I wasn't interested in being one of a couple of dozen candidates vying for a job I knew nothing about. So I left. Just walked out. I think I may have even left the Macy's questionnaire with my name on it behind. You might say that nothing had changed. I was still the goofy guy who had waltzed through college with a C+ average and nowhere to go. But I wasn't. I remember Al "Bwana" Bluth telling me to take an aptitude test, which had helped him decide to become a physical therapist. But I never did. In a way, I took my own aptitude test that day, and I knew I wasn't interested in being an associate in a big firm that sold ties and suits and shoes, even though I figured I might end up wearing them in my first job. I wanted to go small. Be part of something that might grow. Maybe have a little more say in the outcome.

Then my father opened a door for me. He got me an interview at a local TV station in their marketing department. They offered me a job, and I took it. And the next one, which was a nice promotion, to be the head of marketing for the station. We hired a consultant who taught me a ton about sticking to your guns when others are saying you are wrong about the advertising message you are creating. His name was George Rodman, and he made a difference in my life in a very real way. What was great about that experience was that here was a guy who was telling my bosses the same things I'd been saying. But he was a "consultant." Not some kid just out of college like me. They believed him! And he had some successes under his belt. Someone once said that a consultant is really just "an expert from out of town." I started behaving more like an expert. And things changed. The more I acted like an expert (within reason), the more things kept changing.

ABC Television heard my name, I guess, and offered me a job in New York. I respectfully turned them down. It seemed like it was going to be a lot like the job I might have gotten at Macy's. A cog-in-a-wheel kind of job. So, I started courting Bob Fotheringham, who eventually asked me to join his small three-person ad agency. Years later, when we had about 25 people, I left for another opportunity and eventually ended up in sports marketing and sponsorship sales for the Utah Jazz. Lots of things happened in between. It wasn't an even ride. And I didn't make it to the top, for whatever it's worth. But I loved what I did. Small things that make a difference.

My favorite times involved working on a team with a singular mission. Trying to affect change. Trying to achieve something we could feel good about. Passing milestones. Winning a battle. I loved working shoulder to shoulder with my team developing a strategy, and then coming together in a relatively small group to make something worthwhile happen.

As I went along, things kept changing. I was fortunate to play it out, and end up walking away from my final job at the right time. That's one thing I learned. Not to get too complacent, or too relaxed when a battle is won. Because the next battle is right around the corner, and if you don't pay attention, things will change right underneath you, and you won't be ready for it. Change is inevitable. Like the time the house burned down at 51 North Wolcott. It took years for the wiring to wear out so that one little spark could light up a hundred Coors six-pack cartons nailed to the bedroom wall on the second floor. Poof.

Boy, did things change that night!

FIFTY-THREE

Two More Lessons

MY MOTHER TAUGHT me two things that I've drawn from over the years. She did it when she was mad at me for not living up to who she thought I could be.

First, she scolded me one day as a very young boy, when I neglected to say hello or even acknowledge a fellow classmate standing next to me. She watched it happen, and then told me in the car on the way home from school that I needed to change that. "Don't ignore anyone," she said in very harsh terms. She added that since I had no idea what was going on in his world, that maybe a smile and a little cheering up from me would have made a difference in his life that day.

The second thing she taught me came as a result of another scolding. This time I was in high school. I was a typical teenager, prone to moping around the house once in a while when the universe seemed at odds and not giving me all the love and attention I thought I deserved. She watched for a time, and then pulled me aside. I can't remember much of what she said. But the phrases "get going," "take charge of your life," "stop feeling sorry for yourself," and "do it today," were all mixed into her very direct message. Out of those two experiences, over time

I made some conclusions that have helped me become what I hope is a better person.

One of the things I began to realize was that having confidence is just the flip side of not having confidence. With a little effort, we can choose confidence and be a lot happier. I know, it sounds easy. But it really isn't. It took me some time, some mistakes and some setbacks to begin to add a degree of confidence to my disposition and ultimately my demeanor. I'm not 100 percent confident 100 percent of the time, for sure. But I ask myself occasionally, *why not work at choosing the better path of believing in yourself and having a little confidence?*

I also try to make each day special. Take charge, in other words, instead of waiting for something good to come along. I like what John Wooden, the legendary Hall of Fame coach of UCLA said, and I wrote it down: "Make each day your masterpiece." It's true that not every day is a masterpiece, due to circumstances beyond our control, but many situations are controllable. We can make a difference, even a little one. Now we're on our way to having a masterpiece of a day, which is what I think Wooden might have been getting at.

My mom was also a very good golfer. Played on some teams around town in various competitions. She said a couple of things relating to golf that have helped me, too. "Course management" was her big thing. "Why should you hit a shot behind a bunker when you can hit it on the side of it, and give yourself a much better chance of chipping onto the green?" she always said. "Course management" rings in my ears. It's an extension of the concept that you should take control of your life and give yourself more chances to score. Unfortunately, I still shank a shot or two and end up behind the sand trap instead of on or in front of the green. But I love the concept. I'm working to improve my golf game and the other game we all play, the game of life.

The other thing she did very well in golf was concentrate. On every shot. She was good at committing to making the best shot rather than cowering behind a sand trap in despair. She also told me to concentrate on the "next shot" rather than lamenting over the one I had just taken. That one is behind you, and now it's time to prepare for the most important shot of your life, the very next one.

My mother had a dysfunctional childhood. It haunted her, and she struggled to put it behind her. But she never quit, and she eventually won out in that battle. Winston Churchill, in his famous speech supposedly given at his alma mater, Harrow School in 1941, said "never give in" over and over again before sitting down. It was just about the only thing he said, which would make it a pretty easy speech to write. He gave that speech during World War II, so he could speak from experience. There were a lot of dark moments during the war, and many of Winston's cohorts said that maybe they should give up and just sign a nice treaty with Hitler. It was an important war to win, in retrospect, and so are the little wars, or the obstacles we come across every day, in our own lives. Let's stay after it.

FIFTY-FOUR

What Matters

I BECAME BEST FRIENDS with my future wife on our first date, which worked out really well because I was crazy about the way she was put together. Physically. Emotionally. Intellectually. She even had a subtle spirituality, an "aura" you might say, that also drew me to her. I thought very early on, *she's the complete package.* I liked her sense of humor. I liked the way she dressed, stylish but not overstated. I liked the clarity in her eyes. She didn't wear a lot of makeup. She didn't take herself, or anybody else including me, too seriously. She was very content to be herself. Self-contained, you might say. She laughed easily. Giggled, actually, and when she did her voice got a little higher. She carried herself with a nice degree of surety. She was very easy to be around, even though she exuded some spunkiness. On our first date I told her we should kiss goodnight, at least. She took me up on it, reluctantly, I think. The next time I saw her was on a Saturday afternoon when I unexpectedly dropped by her house while she was washing her yellow Triumph Spitfire, wearing a pair of cut-off shorts. That sort of sealed the deal for me. Icing on cake. On our next date, watching a boring movie in some theater, I asked her if we should "neck for a while." She giggled, and I thought her eyes sparkled a little, even in the dark, but that's all that happened.

I was dating other girls at the time. She was dating other guys. We even saw each other with different dates at a movie theater not long after we first started hanging out together. Since I was eleven years older, we agreed to be just friends on our first date. Five months later we got married.

My wife is a perfect example of how people can overcome very difficult circumstances. Not just in marriage, mind you. She was raised by a loving mother, but her father took his own life when she was 12. Before he did that, he was overtly abusive to his wife. Her two sisters and brother were probably in the line of fire, at least a little. Since she was the youngest, she may have escaped some but not all of her father's un-fatherly behavior. Still, she watched.

They all lived in a small house with one bedroom. The three girls slept in the dining room in triple bunk beds. Her brother slept on the back porch, converted into a semi-bedroom. Her father was an untrusting man who had trouble keeping a job and wouldn't let his wife drive a car. If one of the children got sick, she would have to drag a little red wagon to school to pick them up.

Tamie had a close inner circle of friends, but there were others who became distant when they found out where she lived, in a slightly dilapidated neighborhood that seemed out of place in its east side location. That didn't slow her down. She put herself through school, teaching underprivileged children with behavioral disorders, and worked to earn enough money to buy that yellow Triumph Spitfire and the cut-off blue jean shorts to go with it. For the record, I liked her shorts more than her sports car. I think studying behavioral education at the university may have helped her understand me a little better.

Anyway, that's what matters to me most of all. My relationship with my wife. We've been married over forty years now, and I've never looked back. I don't think she has, either.

Next comes our children. They matter most, too, and rank just a half notch behind my wife in importance. That's only because without Tamie and me getting together, where would they be? As parents, we've learned that each of them is uniquely themselves. We love them for who they are and who they are becoming. We stopped trying to make them be something we thought they should be. They became even better than we planned. Sometimes it's difficult not handing out unsolicited advice, especially when they have done something we think, based on our experience, might not be productive for them in the long run. But we've learned. They self-correct; they get back on the horse. I see it in their actions every day. I see a lot of Tamie in them. Once, when I asked my father for advice when I thought the world was going in the wrong direction, he simply said, "Just take care of your family. That's most important. Everything else will take care of itself." I took him to heart on that.

Before I met my wife, one of my goals was to have a good relationship with myself. That took some time. I kept fumbling on the 10-yard line, you might say. Sometimes it was ten yards before the goal, and sometimes it seemed like I was ninety yards away from the end zone. To all the girls I dated and loved during that time: You dodged a bullet. I wasn't ready for you.

But you probably knew that already.

Next comes my belief in God. It's not easy understanding who God is. You can argue "for or against," a line my father used sometimes when a serious topic like this came up. Believing in God doesn't fit everyone. Most of us have a spiritual side to our lives, even if the concept of a God doesn't sit well. I believe in a God who loves us and will welcome us with open arms if we strive to live a good life, treating others like we would want them to treat us. I once read the best way to find God is by serving your fellow men. I like that. Ultimately, how we connect with the Universe is a very personal and individual thing, but an important philosophical question worth looking into.

Of course, it's important to get an education or some training, and then choose a profession so we can give life our best shot. I don't think it really matters what our careers look like, from driving a bus to running a corporation. We can all take pride in our work, no matter what it is. During our working years, if we can live below our means a little, we can be more prepared for the day we walk away and do some other things we'd like to do. That's #5 on my lifelong "To Do" list, if you're counting. I think I got a little lucky in this area, thanks to the advice of some very good friends, so you may not want to ask me to tutor you.

A primary goal in my life is to become the best version of me that I can. I'm not much interested in settling for just a C+ grade anymore. I think I can do better. To help me, I've written myself a sort of personal progress checklist to supplement the other things I've talked about that matter most to me. These include: improving my intellect; staying fit and active; building lifelong friendships with people I admire; having a couple of hobbies I can get absorbed in when there isn't anything else to do; and finally, finding time to do absolutely nothing whenever I'm fed up with a hobby or just get tired of trying to be my best self. That gets old, too.

I would love to make a difference in the lives of others, like Bill Gates or some of the other great philanthropic geniuses do regularly. But maybe I can do a few things here and there to help out and make my immediate world a better place to live. We're in this together, no matter who we are, where we come from or what we look like. Let's lift each other up. Let's do what my dad always said, "level the playing field" a little. We all want the same thing, pretty much: A chance.

Well, there it is. Simple, in theory. Life is a whirlwind of experiences, full of ups and downs, and challenges that seem to come out of nowhere. Happiness—pure good old-fashioned happiness—is out there. And, it's in the moment. I figured that out when I was hanging with my Pi Kapp brothers at 51 North Wolcott.

But you probably knew that already.

*   *   *

Afterword

A FEW WEEKS BEFORE the Pandemic of 2020 started, I went to Founder's Day, a Pi Kappa Alpha reunion party. They touted remodeling the current Pi Kapp house, making sure the wiring was done perfectly. About 75 alumni members attended, from all the way back in the late Fifties to present day. Ross Anderson, our chapter advisor back then, was there. So was Jim Cannon, the house president who helped things change in a big way when we won our chapter title back after pledging Dennis Miya, the first-ever Asian member of any Pi Kappa Alpha chapter. The dinner and speeches that followed helped me remember what a great thing Pi Kappa Alpha had been for my personal development. It's hard to put into words how much all the little, seemingly inconsequential moments I spent with my brothers shaped me as a person, helping me see what an amazing thing the human race really is. And how lucky I had been to be part of something that was dedicated to making a difference in the lives of others. So, I just took it all in, letting the spirit emanating from the men around me just linger. Even though I didn't know everyone there, I felt a connection. I was glad I had become part of something bigger than me.

During dinner, I sat between Bob Bernick, the now retired investigative reporter, and Bill Souvall, a former SMC of the house, too. Bill had made sure his family belonged to Pi Kappa Alpha, including his brothers and sons, all PIKEs. Bill may have been the guy who wallpapered the bedroom at the original Pi Kappa Alpha residence with discarded Coors cartons. He just didn't know about the spark that would occur a few years later from faulty wiring in the makeshift area of the house we called "Siberia," or that it would leap over to those beer cartons.

Luckily, the only thing that burned up that night was the house.

The Pi Kappa Alpha Pledge Class Of 1965 – Alpha Tau Chapter

Scott Anderson
Steve Anderson
Thomas Buxton
Richard Evershed
Michael Healy
Fred Jones
Joseph Karren
Steven Keller
Gary Lund
Richard Lybert
Edward Muir
Rich McClure
Scott Miller
John Nelson
John Nordquist

Wayne Petty
Don Pugh
Doug Richards
Pat Roylance
Terry Rushton
William Smart
Lee Smith
Michael Snarr
Richard Stevenson
Steven Strong
Jeffrey Swinton
Michael Weilenmann
Randy Wright
Craig Zwick

APOLOGIES

The funny thing is, I never really kept notes, or at least very many for the writing of this book. But I always wanted to write it. I kept telling others at the fraternity while we were in the middle of our college careers, spending most of our days in the living room of the frat house rather than a classroom at the university, "someone needs to write a book about all of this." I didn't know it would be me. Many thanks to all you brothers I crossed paths with from 1965 to 1972 and beyond. And, at the same time, Apologies. There were so many more stories to tell. Even as is, it's such an imperfect treatment, this view from one guy who certainly didn't see the big picture, and didn't remember everything in the way many of you did. It was my perspective, and I'm sure it's seen by many of you as extremely narrow and incomplete.

The other thing is, I couldn't find many of you so you could recant what I wrote. I know you're out there, woven into the fabric of the universe, and doing good things. I wish we could have reunited somehow so we could just check in with each other and catch up. And have you spell check me a little. Phi-Phi-K-A

APPRECIATION

Some business executive said, "surround yourself with people who are better than you." I've done that as long as I can remember. It might be my greatest accomplishment. I'll start with Tamie, my beautiful wife of over 40 years, who is my world. She's also editor in chief of this book. She's not only an excellent grammarian, she has perspective. Invaluable. She saw things in between the lines of copy that I didn't. Her opinions and guidance have been instrumental in bringing the entire project to its end game. It's an end game I'm rather proud of, despite its many flaws, generated purely by the author.

Next is Glade and Debbie Curtis. Glade has written a dozen or more medical books and has been published all around the world. Many times over. We're not in the same league, but he was kind enough to give this a thorough look, adding his editing skills and thoughts to every page. Not to mention extensive fact checking. He was the first to read it, and courageously, he read it a second time. His wife, Debbie, a cute Chi Omega from my university, also read and approved of it. I needed that. A witness, to some degree. Thank you both for your wonderful friendship, not to mention your skills.

I want to thank Dave Boyce, my lifelong friend who seems to overlook my weaknesses on and off the golf course, for reading the entire book even though he is a Beta. And, my dear sister Patty, a consummate student of life, for constant encouragement while reading along with me. And, Charlotte Cook, who would read a few chapters and send me an email the next day requesting more. All the way to the finish line. She and her husband, Phil, are special friends even though he had better things to do than read my book. I'm going to read it to him now! Sort of my own audio book rendition, if you will. He says he can't wait. Chris Merrick, my amazing sister-in-law, also a published author, read it to her husband, Randy (Tamie's brother) before he passed. He was an exceptional human being. We loved him completely. Our great friends, Doug and Janet Todd, Val and Jeanne Christensen and Grant and Gay Harrison said to keep going, too. Maybe they thought I needed more to do.

So many others have contributed: Steve Anderson, Lew Bautista, Steve Bushnell, JR Knight, Marilyn Matheson (Roylance), Linda Muhlestein Terry, John Nelson, Charlie

Seldin, Glenn Holley and especially Scott Welling, who remembered lots of things, including a few that are on the editing floor, and Rex "U Haul" Johnson, who is the main character. "Main" being an understatement. There wouldn't be as compelling a reason to write this book if he didn't do what he did. And, thanks, posthumously, to Pat Roylance and Erv Terry for really defining brotherly love. I still miss you guys. We weren't done yet.

Tamie found Gatekeeper Press, who became our publisher. Thanks to all of those involved, especially Jennifer Clark, Jason Pettus, and others who guided us through the process.

Lastly, my heart-filled gratitude to four wonderful children, their significant others, and our first grandchild, a voracious reader of books, who are also my world. They inspire me every day, and act like they like me, too. What could be better than that?